MY VIEW OF SHAKESPEARE

My View of
SHAKESPEARE

The Shakespeare Revolution

A.L. Rowse

Duckworth

First published in 1996 by
Gerald Duckworth & Co. Ltd.
The Old Piano Factory
48 Hoxton Square, London N1 6PB
Tel: 0171 729 5986
Fax: 0171 729 0015

A catalogue record for this book is available
from the British Library

ISBN 0 7156 2746 5

Typeset by Ray Davies
Printed in Great Britain by
Redwood Books Ltd, Trowbridge

Dedicated to
HRH the Prince of Wales
in our common devotion
to William Shakespeare

*'The monarchy and Shakespeare are
the two greatest assets this country
has in the world.'*

Contents

Preface

MOST OF my working life has been spent on research into, and writing about, the Elizabethan Age. So it was only natural that I should embark at length on the life and work of its greatest writer.

Nor should it be surprising that I have been able to make discoveries about both, which amount – it has been said – to a 'revolution' in our knowledge of Shakespeare.

And about time too! For, as Harold Macmillan wrote, *à propos* of my original biography, 'What a mess they have made of it!' 'Experts' like E.K. Chambers and Professor Dover Wilson never noticed that Mr W.H. was the publisher's dedicatee, *not* the young Lord so clearly depicted within the Sonnets – the obvious person, the lordly young patron, Southampton. As Agatha Christie wrote knowingly, 'Everybody misses the significance of the obvious.'

Practically all my solutions to the Shakespeare problems are obvious common sense, when gone into with the historian's proper equipment of dating, an intimate knowledge of events of the time, and with the necessary literary perception of a practising poet. No one hitherto had had this double equipment. Hence the revolution foreshadowed in the first biography. If the solutions worked out therein had not been absolutely, if cautiously, correct I should never had made the later unexpected discoveries. They were a bonus for sticking to my line against all discouragements from the ignorant, the imperceptive and the obtuse – different categories unwilling to learn.

It was not to be expected that ordinary-minded 'experts' would know that, in the Elizabethan Age, it was regular social usage to refer to a knight as 'Mr', and the *rule* in Parliament. Only a social historian would know that. But common sense should have told Chambers, Dover Wilson and all the lesser fry that 'Mr' could never have referred to a Lord.

It was always obvious – though no one saw it – that Mr W.H. was one in the immediate circle of the patron, i.e. his stepfather, Sir William Harvey, from whom the publisher Thomas Thorp (T.T.) got the manuscripts. The dedication, years after the Sonnets were written, had confused everybody, until I worked it out patiently, phrase by phrase.

Similarly with the nature of the Sonnets. Many people not acquainted with the flowery language of the Elizabethans have supposed these dutiful, deferential, affectionate poems from a poet to a generous young patron to be homosexual, though Shakespeare specifically says, in Sonnet 20, that he has no interest in the young man sexually. And everything shows, in both Shakespeare's life and work, that he was exceptionally responsive to women, a normal family man at Stratford, if overstepping the bounds in his London life. Everything in his life is consistent with his work. So that it is merely ignorant, though quite usual, to say that we know little about him. The truth is that we now know more about him than about any other Elizabethan dramatist.

People who are supposed to know better have failed in their duty to instruct the journalists of the media as to the facts.

We know so much about him because he was the most *autobiographical* of the dramatists. He was the only one to write his autobiography during those decisive years 1591/2 to 1594, which formed the central experience of his life, influencing so much of his work then and later.

It needs an intimate knowledge of the time, as well as sensitive perception, to bring to light the numerous, often tactfully indirect, references to experiences, of his own and of the life he observed around him, of which the Plays are so full.

Everyone recognises that *The Tempest* was sparked off by the events of the Virginia Voyage of 1609; and that *Macbeth* celebrated the new Scottish dynasty threatened by the Gunpowder Plot of 1605. Similarly the *Henry VI* plays responded to popular interest in the Normandy campaign of 1591. Everybody has recognised in *Henry V* the salute to Essex – Southampton's leader – leaving London for the Irish campaign in 1599. Similar topical references can be read in all the plays – by one with the knowledge of the time to bring them to light.

Very well then: I have been able to show that events near at hand suggested other plays, or events at the time gave him a subject. *Hamlet* is inspired by the subject of the succession to the throne – the question that dominated people's minds, especially Essex's, around 1600, as the Queen neared the end of her reign.

Early on, in *Love's Labour's Lost*, the poet made fun of Southampton's notorious reluctance to marry (and of himself as Berowne). A few years later other characteristics and incidents in Southampton's career inspired *All's Well That Ends Well.* Just as the feud in neighbouring Wiltshire, between Southampton's friends, the Danvers brothers and the Longs, with the murder of the Long heir, gave the starting point for *Romeo and Juliet*. Everybody recognises the agrarian riots of 1608 in Warwickshire and its neighbours in *Coriolanus*.

And so on. The most successful dramatist of the time naturally had acute 'box office' sense. Not to recognise that shows no sense. Such people do not know how real writers write – they write out of their own experience and of what they observe around them, highlighted by human understanding and imagination.

It should also be obvious that Shakespeare was the most historical of dramatists. Over one third, almost one half of his plays have historical subjects, English and Roman, Scottish and from the pre-history of Britain. *Cymbeline* has a further salute to James I and his family, along with the better known tribute to Elizabeth I.

So an historian and poet need make no apology for clearing up the problems, working out the solutions one by one, setting to rights at last the life and work of which such a 'mess' has been made. It all may not have needed what has been called 'the intuitive and divining power of genius'. I am content to claim knowledge and common sense, along with perception.

I

Prologue: Beginnings

IN THE COURSE of my decades of work on Shakespeare I have had plenty of time to think about him: he has been a constant companion of my thoughts. But for the purpose of scholarly work those have taken second place. In my various Shakespeare books I have been tied down to facts. Here, though based entirely on *facts*, Elizabethan scholarship, both historical and literary, I should like to free myself to think about him and his work – for example, what kind of man he was. How did he come to achieve such miraculous creative work?

I have often been asked that question. Here is the place to consider it, free and untrammelled.

In the first place he had a great advantage in being not only an actor, but so completely a man of the theatre. That enabled him to put himself imaginatively inside other people's skin – man, woman or child. Molière, foremost among French dramatists, was such another, a professional actor. But he was supreme only in comedy, where Shakespeare was supreme in tragedy, history, romance and poetry, as well as comedy. Miraculous – it takes some explaining.

Shakespeare was a good actor, but he was not the star of his Company, the Lord Chamberlain's Men. Richard Burbage was the famous star for tragic parts, William Kemp and later Robert Armin for comic parts, the clowns. We are told that Shakespeare sometimes took 'kingly' parts (he was a king indeed), and even the Ghost in *Hamlet*.

Naturally he could not be acting full-time, for he was producer as well. We know exactly what he was like as a producer, for he has told us in detail in his instructions to the actors performing the play put on before the Court, within *Hamlet*. The keynote of his instructions is that his players must act *naturally* – 'suit the action to the word, and the word to the action', hold the mirror up to nature, etc. He is quite scornful of awkward gestures, 'sawing' the air; still more of actors slipping in gags to make stupid members of the audience laugh, taking its mind off the serious argument of the play.

Evidently with him the *art* of the theatre came first and last – contrary to the age-old misconception of him as a naif 'child of nature'. Nothing naif about *him*! It is obvious, too, that as actor and producer he stood for a more subtle, and supple, kind of acting than the earlier Elizabethan rhetorical style, stomping about the stage like Marlowe's Tamburlaine. There *is* rhetoric at command in Shakespeare, but in keeping with the play's demand for it, the character part. As his work progresses so this becomes clearer: once more we see the *artist* in control, the artistic determination dominant.

Then there was theatrical business. Earlier on he took care of the takings – he was careful about money, unlike his father, a jolly old fellow. From 1594 when William was thirty – already middle-aged in those days – he became a founder member of the Lord Chamberlain's Company, a part-sharer in its takings. Later, from 1608 – at forty-four – he became part-owner of the Blackfriars Theatre. Nobody was ever more completely a man of the theatre than he was.

He had not intended that earlier on. In the Elizabethan Age it was much more highly regarded to be a poet. To be an actor purely and simply was a low profession, and the ambitious William resented the necessity. However, he was not only an actor, he was a poet as well – and proceeded to make the best of both. Further, his long and successful career in the theatre had the most important effect in elevating the profession. When James I came to the throne he took the Companies under the patronage of the royal family. The Lord Chamberlain's Men became the King's

Men, and Shakespeare a Groom of the Chamber, in recognised royal service.

The circumstances of the time were extremely propitious to his ascent and that of his profession. The theatres in London became a prime attraction, not only for Londoners and visitors from the country, but for tourists from abroad. The English drama had the wholly unexpected, the astonishing fortune to become the first in Europe. There was nothing comparable in the contemporary closet drama in France, the bookish Senecan drama of Garnier (translated by Philip Sidney's sister). Sidney himself, though herald and precursor of the new literature, had no idea of the prodigious potentialities of the vernacular drama.

It was a veritable explosion, when one considers the depths of passion it expressed and released, the cross-fertilising fusion of history with tragedy, both with comedy and satire, knockabout farce, questionable topicalities – all the profusion, at its height in the 'miraculous fecundity' of Shakespeare, which so much vexed Voltaire, restricted to the regularities of French classical models.

I. Prologue: Beginnings

To what was such an unparalleled explosion of genius and talent due?

There can be no simple literary answer to such a question, no explanation in terms of literature itself. The historian may help by pointing to the inspiration of the age. It was one of historic expansion by land and sea across the oceans to new worlds of discovery. This was visibly reflected in the realms of the mind. The language itself was in a pregnant, proliferating condition, filling itself out with new words and phrases – naturally to accommodate the intellectual expansion – notably from Latin and Greek as well as contemporary foreign languages.

Something of this parallel movement, of body and mind, I have portrayed in *The Expansion of Elizabethan England* carried over into *The Elizabethan Renaissance*. For it was indeed a Renaissance of its own kind, the profusion due to the fertilising of Gothic substance with classic influences. One *sees* this as much in the architecture and art of the age, in the soaring roofscapes of Longleat or Hardwick, Wollaton or Hatfield, as in the battlements and crevices of *Hamlet* or *King Lear*, *Antony and Cleopatra* or *Troilus and Cressida*.

All this witnessed to, was indeed the result of, a similarly unparalleled explosion of talent, very striking when compared with the barrenness of the mid-sixteenth century. Very variegated it was too – notice-ably in its sexuality – to anyone familiar with the sex-life of the age. When one thinks of its ambivalence and ambidexterity, it is rather comic to think of the Virgin Queen giving her name to it. The matrimonial tangles of her prime favourite, Leicester, made history. So did those of his successor, Ralegh, or of several of the Queen's vulnerable maids-of-honour (Mary Fitton was a notorious example), whose 'honour' was in his keep-ing as Captain of the Guard.

For all William Shakespeare's known affair with the dark young lady of the Sonnets, he was really a family man, with his ambition to set up as a country gentleman in his native Warwickshire. Denizens of literary Bohe-mia were very different: Robert Greene, deserting a wife to live with a prostitute; Christopher Marlowe, famously homosexual, a proselytiser for his inclinations; Francis Bacon and his brother Anthony, both similarly inclined (Anthony had a narrow escape from dangerous prosecution for sodomy in France). Southampton, Wil-liam's patron, was homo when young: even after his reluctant marriage in 1598, which turned out happily; he was not averse to fumblings with the braggadocio Captain Edmond, in his tent during the campaign in Ireland in 1599. The Earl of Oxford was married to Burghley's daughter, but treated her badly, and preferred his Italian page. James I was introduced to the ambivalent pleasures of Henri III's Court, by his cousin Esmé Stuart, and thereafter had a succession of boy-friends, James Hay, Robert Carr, and George Villiers, handsomest man of his day.

All this meant nothing to William Shakespeare: it was not in his line. It was a great advantage to him as a writer to be so responsive to the other sex, to be deeply sympathetic to female nature and understand it inti-mately (like Tolstoy or Turgenev). He did not have the cock-eyed view of life, the proportions distorted, as in so many modern writers, Proust and Gide, Monther-lant and Cocteau. He made no apology for his well-known 'sportive blood', as he phrased it.

The sportive young fellow acquitted himself well in giving Anne Hathaway a child when he was eighteen and a half, she a woman some seven or eight years older – and that meant more in those days. The Hathaways, of Hewlands farm a mile or so out of Stratford, were of the same social standing as the Shakespeares at the upper end of town – good yeomen middle-class stock. The families were acquainted. The Hathaway farm, like others around Stratford, grew rye – and 'in the acres of the rye those pretty country folks did lie'? In Elizabethan days the very word 'country' had a sexual reference, as we know from a bawdry phrase of Hamlet to Ophelia.

Since the lady was some months pregnant, the young fellow hurried on the wedding by special licence. So the eldest child, Susanna, was born legitimate, the clever one of the family, who turned after her youthful parent. Twenty months later Anne gave birth to twins, Judith and Hamnet, given the name of a neighbour in Henley Street, Hamnet Sadler (actually Hamnet and Hamlet are the same name, interchangeable).

The young husband was sportive in other directions too. We know that he was keen on archery; the butts were at the bottom end of town, in the meadow by Clopton's bridge. Also bowls – a rather select game then; and he knew about falconry and coursing the hare up on the Cotswolds.

Most of all, he was keen on hunting the deer – as we can tell from his absolute obsession with it in all his early work, poems and plays alike. There was nothing criminal in that, though it was a sueable offence and liable to lead to trouble. Oxford graduates would take a day off to hunt the Queen's deer up in Shotover Forest (much more extensive in those days, when Milton's Catholic grandfather was the keeper).

There clearly was a spot of trouble about their deer with the Puritanical Lucys out at Charlecote, for later on in a play there is a joke against the Lucys and their coat of arms, luces – not unfriendly, certainly not malicious. That would not be like him, he was no satirist (unlike Ben Jonson), much more of a romantic.

It all adds up to the picture of a lively young countryman – Stratford-upon-Avon was a busy country town – very much in touch with the fun-fairs and frolics going on, cattle market and parish feasts, May Day and maypoles, to which Puritans so much objected. They understood their Freudian significance, what they stood for and what went on around them. Then there were shearing feasts out on the Cotswolds, recalled in *A Winter's Tale* years later. Or we have a lovely, throwaway phrase, 'the morning star calls up the shepherd'. It is all very different from Marlowe and Ben Jonson, both townees – one attending King's School, Canterbury, the other Westminster School.

Young William had the same sort of education at Stratford Grammar School, for in Elizabethan days grammar school education was the same all over the country, largely out of Lilly's Latin Grammar, father of the playwright, John Lyly. Actually, there is more about grammar school education and how it was conducted, chiefly in Latin, in several of the plays, than in any other dramatist of the time. There is a further reason for this: for a short time the young man, we learn, taught school in the country. That too shows itself in the way the earliest plays are indebted to school texts, Plautus, Ovid, Julius Caesar, a bit of Seneca. Somewhat surprisingly, there is too a strongly didactic note in the plays: the mature man moralises as much as Dr Johnson, though not such a strict moralist in the conduct of his life. Evidently strongly sexed, he was no Puritan. Also a handsome, well-favoured man – and to be well-favoured is 'a gift of fortune'. Fortunate again! He did not go on to the university (unlike Marlowe): why should he? – his was the university of life.

Church-going was a very important part of one's education. Everybody had to go on Sundays and on the chief feasts of the Church, or there would be trouble. That he was regularly attentive we can tell from how strongly and frequently the phrases of Morning and Evening Prayer are quoted, particularly in the early plays, and from the Prayer Book version of the Psalms. Though the chancel at Holy Trinity was closed off then, how cold it must have been in that large parish church, in winter when 'coughing drowns the parson's saw'! All the children were, like himself (26 April 1564), baptised in the font – damaged later by the destructive Puritans, as we can see today.

William had no liking for them, any more than the Queen had. With his attachment to old customs and folklore, old ways and habits, he had a friendly feeling for the old faith and its relics – the term 'priest' is as frequent with him as 'parson', or 'by the Mass', not yet out of date. In the variegated, colourful society of the town – on the way to Wales, Welsh cattle drovers, Fluellens, coming in and out – there were Catholics and Catholic sympathisers left, neighbours with whom he was friendly.

The Bible was no less important, and it is noticeable that he was particularly taken by Genesis and the stories of the Creation, Adam and Eve, Cain and Abel. Again, from the Bishops' Bible in use in church; later in life he took to the Geneva Bible, of convenient pocket size. Altogether his schooling with its induction into Latin – no Greek – provided a sufficient foundation; as with other men of genius his education was self-education and came later. He was a constant reader, who read rapidly, as he did everything – writing too – keeping his eye on the books and pamphlets coming out in London for anything he could make use of. With him everything was grist to the mill.

The family were settled in the house at the top of Henley Street – now famous as the birthplace, and not entirely changed. Within is the little hall with large open fireplace, above is the big chamber, scene of births and deaths. Beyond the house was then open country, and at the back – now a garden full of the poet's favourite flowers – a yard where the cattle would be killed. For John Shakespeare was a glover, who needed their skins – the son knew all about the business, down to the softest cheveril, deerskin, for gloves. We learn at the same time from his words his sympathy for the poor beasts. There was a little pentice to the shop front. The father also had a standing at the market cross at the bottom of the street, the crossroads where the western road leads to the Gild Chapel, the Grammar School, and so around to Holy Trinity church. Up along from there was the Rother (i.e. Cattle) Market – and 'it is the pasture that lards the rother's sides.'

Someone handed on the view of John Shakespeare as a merry-cheeked old boy, not loth to crack a joke with his celebrated son. He too was a merry fellow – 'a merrier man I never met withal' was his own view of himself – with an infinite store of wit and bawdy jokes. In that way very much the sexy heterosexual – homosexuals naturally are not given to that sort of joke (Marlowe, for example).

John Shakespeare had come into the town from the country out at Snitterfield. He had made a good marriage, to Mary Arden, a small heiress owning some land of her own. John was an up-and-coming fellow who took to town life and went through the whole course of civic offices until he ended prominently as bailiff, equivalent to mayor, of Stratford. It is clear that he neglected his business for the town's, going up to London on occasion for it. In spite of his good start, he became embarrassed with debt, and had to mortgage his wife's inheritance to her relations, the Lamberts. When the son eventually prospered he once and again tried to get his mother's inheritance back – in vain.

The town recognised his father's services, for the council excused him the fines for non-attendance at meetings. Even more humiliating, John could not show up at church 'for fear of process for debt' – and hence was liable to fines for recusancy: quite disparaging enough without supposing him to have been a Catholic. Nor had the eldest son been much of a help in getting tied up to a woman without a dowry – she fairly certainly couldn't write – and finding himself at twenty-one with a wife and three children to support.

This was the more humiliating because the young

31

man was family-proud, particularly of his mother's family, Ardens of the Forest of Arden, and an ambitious fellow, anxious to make a good show in the town where they were prominent, and now down on their luck.

One must give reasons. It was not until the foundation of the Lord Chamberlain's Company, when William was already thirty, that his feet were on firm ground and he achieved security. He at once sued out a coat of arms, but in his father's name, so that he should have been born an armigerous gentleman, and citing family services to the Crown – though nobody knows what, if any, they were. Evidently someone, not the father, was drawing the longbow – the son was good at that. Look at the motto *'Non sans droit'*, Not without right, indeed.

Ben Jonson laughed at him for this exercise, and suggested a boar's head on a charger for a coat, the motto to be 'Not without mustard'. Nothing daunted, a couple of years later William tried to impale these arms with those of the gentry family, the Ardens of Park Hall in North Warwickshire. But this the College of Arms disallowed.

It was very important to him to be recognised as a gentleman, and in this he was markedly successful. He was frequently denoted as 'gentle', in the Elizabethan usage for gentlemanly, and regularly later as 'Master

Shakespeare'. We may note that this is confirmed by his courteous addresses to the audience in Prologues and Epilogues – such a contrast to Ben Jonson's abrasive idiom. It is borne out by the whole conduct of his life – conspicuously one of the few theatre folk to behave prudently, tactfully and never get into trouble. Ben Jonson killed a fellow actor, Marlowe got himself killed, several others similarly, or were in and out of prison. William Shakespeare never.

The emphasis on gentility is very noticeable, particularly in the earlier plays. All this has its sociological significance in the circumstances of the time. It would be anachronistic to use the modern word 'snobbish', for in an hierarchical society, yet of marked mobility, men of ability wanted to move upward. They valued independence, as he did; such a society offered incentives and rewarded initiative. Francis Drake, a poor boy with just a small boat on the Medway, ended up as the most famous Englishman of the day, perhaps in all the world. William Shakespeare, after considerable struggle with adverse circumstances, achieved what he meant to be, an independent country gentleman, based in Stratford with property, lands, rents, tithes, within and without the parish. Shortly after he began to make money in London he bought himself the finest house in Stratford. Other successful theatre men, his colleagues Heming and Condell, invested in London property. Not so Shakespeare; he set up his rest – to use an Elizabethan phrase – in his native town where his family had suffered a serious set-back, and some humiliation. Perhaps that acted as a spur to ambition.

Gentility had too its practical use. If he had not been a gentleman he would not have found it easy to be accepted in the aristocratic circle of the young Earl of Southampton. Here he found his full, true nature, perhaps we may say, discovered it for himself.

Meanwhile life was harsh, circumstances were adverse, he had an uphill struggle, a family to maintain with no easy means of support. What was he to do?

Like other men with talents to dispose of, some men of genius – like the young schoolmasterly Samuel Johnson with the play *Irene* in his pocket – the married William took the road to London.

II

The Southampton Circle

WE KNOW that William was in Stratford in 1587, the year the twins were born; after that, fairly certainly away, for there are no further evidences of him at home for some years. He had his living to get: no prospects there, with the whole family in depressed circumstances.

From what he tells us later himself, when things were looking up, he much resented the necessity of earning his living as an actor, when he preferred to be a fine gentleman. In those early days the actors' was a very ungentlemanly profession: the law classed them as vagrants.

They formed at first small amateur groups of half-a-dozen men, not much more, who recommended themselves to the protection of some grandee and took his name – Leicester's, Derby's, Pembroke's, Lord Strange's, Hunsdon's, the Lord Admiral's. They got a step up in 1583 when the Queen's Men came together, a dozen of the best men selected from the groups. Leicester's Men ended in 1588 after his death, worn out by the strain of organising an army and defence against the Armada in case the Spaniards landed.

The little acting groups toured round the country, as we see from the various town records that have survived. In London they had playing places, usually inn-yards with their convenient galleries about, like the New Inn at Gloucester, or the George in Southwark. In London, in the City itself, the Corporation was consistently hostile, and the players needed the favourable protection of Queen and Court. When eventually a couple of permanent theatres were built – by the Burbages, of Warwickshire background, who were Lord Hunsdon's Men – the buildings, the Theatre and the Curtain, were outside the City's jurisdiction, in Shoreditch. Later, the Burbages transferred their theatre to Southwark and built the Globe, again beyond the Corporation's arm.

When first in London William lodged, we are told, in Shoreditch where theatre folk, musicians, poets and such people lived. We hear of Marlowe, as usual in trouble, there – in a fray, his comrade the poet and madrigalist Watson killing his man. We hear no more of William than the tradition of his holding horses outside the Theatre. Need we believe that? No reason against it, for it comes down through the poet William

Davenant, who liked to be thought William's by-blow
– as he may well have been.

What is certain is that Shakespeare's first permanent
association was with the Curtain, and that throughout
his career he was associated with the Burbages. We do
not know which of these shifting little groups, if any, he
worked with. However, when he stretched forth his
hand at writing plays, Strange's and Pembroke's
seemed to have some playing rights in them, as with
Marlowe's too. Marlowe had a prodigious early success
with his *Tamburlaine*, immediately on coming down
from Cambridge in 1587. No such luck for William –
nor was Marlowe 'roped and tied' by wife and family as
William was.

Nor had he the luck of George Peele, writing plays
while still at Christ Church, Oxford, or John Lyly, a
Magdalen man, helped by Burghley and taken up by
the Court. Thomas Lodge, a Lord Mayor's son, and
Thomas Kyd, who had a resounding success with *The
Spanish Tragedy* and probably wrote an early *Hamlet*, had
the advantage of being Londoners. So had Edmund
Spenser, of Merchant Taylors' School with its well-
known tradition of school plays and boys' acting. Ben
Jonson's Westminster School had the regular tradition
of Latin plays, which went on right up to our time.

Robert Greene and young Nashe were Cambridge men, like Marlowe.

William Shakespeare had none of these advantages: he was a provincial, with a provincial accent, as we learn from Greene.

Shakespeare was well aware of his disadvantages, as he expressed them with resentment in the Sonnets. However, he always made the most of what he had got, and in every way: it is characteristic of him intellectually, as poet and dramatist, in his business and profession, and socially, as a man.

Stratford brought him a crucial advantage, in the friendship of a fellow townsman, Richard Field, the printer in Blackfriars. The Fields were tanners at home, who naturally had dealings with John Shakespeare the glover. Young Richard was apprenticed to the well-known Huguenot printer, Vautrollier, and when he died, Richard married the widow with the press.

Ambitiously he struck out not only as printer but as publisher, and a distinctly highbrow one. He published in Latin a fine edition of Ovid's *Metamorphoses*, always Shakespeare's favourite poet and a prime influence in his work, especially in its beginnings. In 1589 Field produced Puttenham's *Art of English Poesy*, on the whole the best critical treatment of the time on the subject. This is the critical work that Shakespeare agreed with – it confirmed his views: they shared sympathy with vernacular forms – and shortly William patented the English form of Sonnet, as against the Italian form used by Surrey, Spenser and Sidney.

More significant were Field's foreign publications, particularly topical tracts and pamphlets on French affairs. When, in a few years, Shakespeare's autobiographical play, *Love's Labour's Lost*, was written the leading characters came from these: Navarre, Longueville, Dumaine (Mayenne), Biron. Note that the Anglicised form Berowne retains the French accentuation; the character is autobiographical, a pleasant skit on the author himself, his tastes and foibles; his fondness for women, for jokes, good food and plenty of sleep. An euphoric, good-tempered personality. The character Don Armado was easily recognisable for the vainglorious Don Antonio Pèrez, Philip II's former Secretary, now a boring exile in the Essex-Southampton circle. Field had also published a Spanish work of his.

We see how much William's work owed to the books coming out from his friend's press, or at hand, in Blackfriars. Whatever else he was doing, he was reading, as always, in these years getting on with his education. It was natural that when the fruits began to appear he should use Field. *Venus and Adonis*, 'the first heir of my invention', was published by him in 1593; next year he printed *The Rape of Lucrece*. *Cymbeline* has a tribute to Field, appropriately in French, Richard du Champ, in 1608. Why? – Because in that year Shakespeare, now highly successful, was back in Blackfriars as part-owner of the private theatre there.

In 1587 appeared the much enlarged edition of Holinshed's *Chronicles*. Now one could read the fascinating stories of the English past, which one never heard at school. There the only history one learned was biblical or Roman, and that on a side-wind for its moral instruction: in this the stories of Cain and Abel and of Julius Caesar made a lasting impression. Reading Holinshed opened up a new, even richer field.

In 1591 the war woke up with a campaign in Normandy to aid Henry of Navarre, led by the Queen's dashing favourite, the young Earl of Essex. His disciple, the Earl of Southampton, as yet only seventeen, scuttled across the Channel, without permission from the Queen, to join in the gallantry and make 'a name in the story'. She strongly disapproved, with her maternal care for the society in her charge, of unmarried peers risking their lives abroad when they had not yet done their duty and begotten heirs to continue their titles. The country too was roused by the campaign in that evocative country: it brought back memories enshrined in the noble old war song, 'Our King went forth to Normandy' ...

Here at last was Shakespeare's chance to put himself across to the public. He seized it with the redoubled, incandescent energy which had been held up for so long. Henceforth it poured forth, undammed, torrentially, in unimpeded creativity. He produced a play on the reign of Henry VI, from his reading of Holinshed, the period of the 'Hundred Years War' with France, and at home the 'Wars of the Roses', the conflicts between York and Lancaster for the throne.

The play was so successful – today we could hail it as a box office triumph – that a sequel was indicated. He was only too ready to oblige, and even with a third play on these themes: we have the complete trilogy today, first of the long succession of plays inspired by English history, which in a sense he had discovered for himself. Those on Roman and early British history came later, to make him the most historically minded of all dramatists.

This was too much for that veteran of literary Bohemia, Robert Greene, whose prose-works were best-sellers; his plays were not so successful. Only thirty-seven, he was now on his death-bed, for he had lived a rakish life, deserting an honest wife, living with a whore, sister of a cut-purse. With his last words he indicted the interloper, the new playwright, in a venomous attack. This has been chewed over and over by the commentators, while they have failed to perceive half the indictment, very revealing in its nasty way.

They have perceived well enough the main charge. Here was a mere player who had the impertinence to turn playwright, challenging the place of university men like Greene himself, to whom actors were indebted for the material they presented. And wasn't this man a plagiarist? Who was he? A few years ago a stroller carrying his fardel (pack) on his back, a bag-man. Now with a fortune in the clothes on his back, in the guise of a gentleman, while only a provincial with an ungracious accent.

He went on to warn his fellow university wits, Marlowe, Peele, Nashe, against the upstart who 'supposes he is as well able to bombast out a blank verse as the best of you.' Greene refers to 'the seven years as absolute interpreter of the puppets' – this takes us back, if reliable, to 1585. Does this indicate the long period in the doldrums, those long years of waiting for a breakthrough? Greene concluded that the new man was 'an absolute Johannes Factotum', able in his own conceit to turn his hand to anything. This was true enough, and a pointer to the future.

William Shakespeare was deeply hurt by this public exposure from a celebrated writer, and in such circumstances. He paid a formal call on Henry Chettle, who had passed it for the press. What stung him most was the aspersions on his social standing, on his not being a gentleman – a university MA was regularly recognised as such. Chettle had not met him but now, in the handsomest apology, was able to say 'myself have seen his demeanour no less civil than he excellent in the quality he professes. Besides, divers of worship have reported his uprightness of dealing, which argues his honesty.'

The word had a stronger (the Latin) sense in those days, it meant that Shakespeare was a good citizen. Chettle had the goodness to add a tribute to 'his facetious [i.e. easy] grace in writing that approves his art'. By this time we know that he was a good actor, we do not know who the 'divers of worship' i.e. gentlemen, were who spoke up for him. Chettle was a friend of Greene; he had never met Shakespeare, who evidently did not consort with literary Bohemia.

The very early *Titus Andronicus* is close to *Henry VI*, but something of a school play, its inspiration coming from

Ovid, its ghastly horrors from Seneca. These appealed to avid Elizabethans and it became a success with them. Not with us, though our enlightened age has seen worse horrors on a larger scale. When the play was put on after our Second German War some of the audience left, sickened. Too near the bone. The playwright was out to be sensational. A touch of modernity occurs with the race-theme. The evil Queen of the piece has a black lover, and is betrayed by her baby proving black. Amid these amenities there are charming insets of the countryside, as if written at Stratford with the Cotswolds in view.

The neighbourhood was recognisably in view in the engaging *The Taming of the Shrew*. This is supposed to be put on before Christopher Sly, made a fool of for the purpose: 'am not I Christopher Sly, old Sly's son of Burton-heath?', i.e. Barton on the Heath, where Shakespeare's uncle and aunt, the Lamberts, lived... 'Ask Marion Hacket, the fat ale-wife of Wincot', near Stratford. There are also Stephen Sly and 'old John Naps of Greet', further out across the Cotswolds. The play is a farce, but it represents what Elizabethans really thought about the relations between husbands and wives – hardly a feminist tract.

II. The Southampton Circle

Had he yet met Southampton? Was he one of the divers of worship, who had testified for him against Greene?

The young Earl, interested in literature and the arts, now back from Normandy, would naturally be interested in the new dramatist sensationally successful with the Normandy plays. The player-playwright was no longer young, as age was told then; in that memorable year of the public insult offered him, 1592, he was twenty-eight and over. Southampton at eighteen would be of age and, the last of his Wriothesley (pronounced Risley) family, it was his duty to marry, beget an heir and carry on the peerage. He was the third Earl.

The family had had its troubles. It was Catholic, and his father had been in the Tower as a foolish supporter of Mary Stuart. He also treated his wife badly, neglecting her for a man-friend, a household servant who ran him and his affairs. He died young, his son – whom we can see as a boy in armour on the grand family tomb at Titchfield near Southampton – left to the care of guardians and his mother.

They were all anxious to get the young man safely married off: his guardian, the great Lord Burghley, his grandfather, the Catholic Lord Montagu, above all his mother. The widowed countess was by all accounts a charming woman, the fact that she was a Catholic did not lose her the Queen's favour. But Elizabeth I did not approve of the son, who again and again entered her bad books, and she would have known all his ways. He was determined to please himself, remain free, and not to be roped and tied into marriage. For some time he remained homoerotic.

It seems that the poet-actor-playwright was called upon in the regular campaign to get the young Earl to marry, for the Sonnets begin with a series of poetic persuasions to that end – also with a graceful tribute to the mother, evidently she approved. The generous young peer, keen to shine in the arts as in action, had taken on the poet as his patron. When the Sonnets were brought to light, the longish poem 'A Lover's Complaint' emerged with the *cache* from the Southampton ambience – evidently the poet's first tribute, with the young patron recognisable in what is a kind of diploma piece. The Sonnets themselves are formally patronage poems, the regular offerings of an Elizabethan poet to his patron – though they offer so much else, constitute a moving dramatic story. It would make a fine play – odd that no one has ever thought of it, but until today it has been mostly misunderstood.

The young man at this time was of a feminine cast of beauty – Renaissance people were as appreciative of beauty in young males as in females – look at the

portraits. There are many of Southampton – 'many
there are that did his picture get' – so that we know
exactly what he looked like at this time. Grey-blue eyes,
fair to auburn-gold hair: he was particularly distinguished by the long love-lock over the left shoulder
which emphasised his femininity.

William was responsive to every kind of beauty, and
wrote of it naturally in a way to appeal to the young
peer's vanity, 'from fairest creatures we desire increase.'
There was no response to this appeal: the young man
was not a marrying sort, unlike his poet, who liked to
see everybody properly coupled up. Nor was his response to the youth at all sexual, as he specifically tells
us. Nature had intended him for a woman, which – if it
had been so – all very well. But Nature had given him
something, which 'me of thee defeated by adding something to my purpose nothing': i.e. a prick. Since he had
been pricked out for women's pleasure, they could have
him, Shakespeare was contented to have his love. We
may add to that, his support, for the poet was in need
of it, and Southampton was properly generous.

It is a subtle matter to catch exactly what William's
feelings were in this stroke of good fortune, at last, no
longer young. In the first place, gratitude for the favour
that lifted him out of the range of insults: 'for what care
I so you o'er-Greene my faults.' That kind of oblique,

tactful reference was to become characteristic. He favoured 'by indirection to find directions out' – so that one needs both the intimacy of contemporary knowledge and a subtle perception to track him down. One needs also a close knowledge of the society of the time and its conventions. There was the proper deference of a gentlemanly poet to an Earl – hence the flowery language which has taken in so many unsubtle people who are not familiar with the custom of that age. When poets addressed the Queen – Shakespeare included – they invoked her as a goddess.

With time and admission to something like friendship the poet's feeling became a kind of love, not erotic, hence difficult to define. It was partly paternal: the young man was without a father's guidance, in the slippery treacheries of the Court, exposed to all the temptations of wealth and arrogant status. 'Dear my love, you know you had a father.' The son had had a good education at Cambridge, in Burghley's college of St John's: he had bookish tastes, and later gave it a consignment of books. So Shakespeare's feeling was in part tutorial – he had, himself a father, a definite feeling of responsibility for the youth's well-being.

This emerges clearly when it fell to him to introduce Southampton to Emilia Bassano, the former mistress of Lord Chamberlain Hunsdon; when pregnant, she was married off to a Court musician, the French Alphonse Lanier. Down on her luck, cast down from her conspicuous position, the inflammable poet fell for her out of pity for her condition – always of appeal to a vulnerable male. She preferred to make a pass at the young Earl – they were of an age, the poet several years older. Emilia, with her Italian-Jewish temperament and cast down from on high, had become promiscuous, known to be so. This worried the older man for the youth's sake, for he had as yet no experience of women and there was the ever-present danger of venereal disease.

Shakespeare was all the more worried because he did not know what was happening with the young people – he was not all that *au fait* with the Earl's domestic life. Clearly Southampton was not trapped, as the older man was, helplessly infatuated with a beautiful, dark young woman with all her attractions, musical, well educated, brought up in the lap of aristocracy – since she too was an orphan – by the Countess of Kent. To this was added the excitement of her being half-foreign, and that Italian, of irresistible charm in the Renaissance world.

This interruption made a rift in the close friendship, and the younger man apologised for his betrayal. He emerged unscathed and was forgiven by his senior; all the same, things had lost the primal innocence of the beginning of this remarkable affair – unparalleled as it became for its literary interest and largely misunderstood by unapt minds for its subtlety.

Shortly there ensued another complication, another challenge to the friendship. This time from another poet, a rival for the Earl's patronage. This was all the more dangerous for Shakespeare was dependent for some support. Particularly in these very years 1592 and 1593 when plague raged fiercely, theatres and playing places closed, acting out of the question. The little companies were badly affected; some took to the country, where one of them – Pembroke's – foundered; Robert Brown went abroad and spent the rest of his career as an actor in Germany. In these years men died like flies.

Shakespeare was all the more endangered because his rival was Christopher Marlowe, whom he recognised as his superior, as everybody else would have done at the time, both as poet and playwright. (He was above being an actor.) As rivals for the Earl's patronage each was engaged on a poem – Shakespeare's *Venus and Adonis*, Marlowe's *Hero and Leander*. A close comparison, which was never made, there was such confusion in this field – shows that the two were well aware of each other's work. There are tell-tale echoes and correspondences of phrase. And in truth Marlowe's work is superior artistically.

Shakespeare recognised this candidly – candour was another characteristic of his, not merely gentlemanly self-deprecation. Marlowe's was 'a worthier pen', his 'precious phrase by all the Muses filed in polished form'. This was true of that 'able spirit', while himself was but an 'unlettered clerk'. His respect for the 'learned' appears: here is the sense of inferiority to the university wits, which Greene had blazoned to the public.

More important, what would happen if Marlowe were to win, 'if he thrive and I be cast away'? 'Your shallowest help will hold me up afloat', otherwise he would be 'wrecked'. Here was a crisis, and in this appalling time of plague!

The rivalry was suddenly resolved: Marlowe was accidentally killed at Deptford, on 2 May 1593, after a day's eating and drinking with his questionable acquaintance, over a tiff about the reckoning. William knew the circumstances, 'a great reckoning in a little room.' He paid tribute to his dead colleague and rival in a fine sonnet to the patron. He signalised 'the proud full sail of his great verse': Marlowe's achievement had been to marry fine poetry to the stage, in this he was the beginner, the 'dead shepherd' Shakespeare called him and was his follower.

Others had tried for the generous patron's support too, young Nashe among them. But they had not been 'victors' of any silence on Shakespeare's part, for he had carried on with his usual persistence, not only with sonnets but with plays to amuse and occupy Southampton's circle.

Sadly, but luckily for his future, those critical years saw a clearance of the field for him. Not only were Greene and Marlowe dead, so too were Thomas Watson, Peele and Thomas Kyd, young Nashe was not long to follow – most of them in their thirties or even late twenties. Such were the unfair chances of life at the time.

Those upsets in the course of friendship – 'the course of true love never did run smooth' – had their consequences. We have a whole sonnet reproaching his young Lord for keeping him waiting, busy as he was – as if he had nothing else to do but 'tend upon the hours and times of your desire', and wait 'until you require'. Time, to Shakespeare, was precious, but, 'being your slave', he had to put up with it and not take account of Southampton's 'times of pleasure'. The poet was at his patron's 'beck', he had to 'bide each check'. We see the two growing apart and note the difference between an actor, however gentlemanly and poetical, and an aristocrat of the time.

In the middle of the period when the poet was doing duty with his lordly young patron with the Sonnets – patronage poems in their inspiration and continuance – we find their story used to make a play. Needs must: he needed to make use of anything and everything ready to hand – and *The Two Gentlemen of Verona* is entirely autobiographical, the story of the two friends in rivalry for the same woman. We are informed that the claims of friendship come first in everything – except in 'the office of love'.

Our special interest is in the specific reference, 'Writers say, as in the sweetest bud the eating canker dwells, so eating love inhabits in the finest wits of all.' This is Shakespeare speaking of himself, with the same image and virtually the same words as in the contemporary Sonnet. To which the younger friend responds, 'and writers say ... even so the young and tender wit is turned to folly, losing all the fair effects of future hopes.' Here was the warning to the youthful peer of promise. 'But wherefore waste I time to counsel thee that art a votary to fond desire?'

The lines referring to Leander swimming the

Hellespont to visit Hero remind us of the other rivalry going forward – that of Marlowe's poem competing with *Venus and Adonis*. And there are lines later on practically interchangeable with others in the Sonnets – the year being 1592.

There followed next *Love's Labour's Lost*. This play was regarded for ages as an insoluble enigma. It is now nothing of the kind, to anyone who knows the facts and circumstances behind it. It is a skit, a farce, on Southampton's reluctance to respond to women. He is the King of Navarre who abjures their society and commands his courtiers to give themselves up to their books. One of them, Berowne, i.e. Shakespeare, takes the opposite line and stands out for women. Men do not learn from books but from the experience of life, especially from female society – 'but love first learnèd from a lady's eye', that is the only academe, we might say university.

Amid the characters of Southampton's circle reflected in the play it is fascinating to have Shakespeare's portrayal of himself as he was at this time, verging on thirty, very recognisable as Berowne (i.e. Navarre's follower, Biron). 'A merrier man' there never was, turning everything he observed to a mirth-moving jest, expressed in 'apt and gracious words'. His 'wit' is the clue, and to Elizabethans this meant intelligence too. For all his courtesy, and deference to his patron, he knew his own quality: one of 'the finest wits of all'.

He goes on to a skit on his own foibles, against the farce of the young courtiers forgoing the company of women. 'Not to see a woman in that term' – absurd. Equally ridiculous to fast one day a week, 'and but one meal on every day beside!' Evidently he liked his food, and a good night's sleep. Only three hours allowed – and 'not to be seen to wink of all the day! – when I was wont to think no harm all night, and make a dark night too of half the day.' We appreciate the innuendo – so characteristic of him.

It all adds up to a sane, normal healthy countryman – such a contrast to the noctivagant Marlowe, the erratic Earl of Oxford, or Francis and Anthony Bacon, devoutly homosexual.

This is brought home to the males by a deputation of ladies from the Court of France. In the train of the Princess is a lady, Rosaline, whom everybody was able to recognise as Shakespeare's Dark Lady, and we can recognise as Emilia Lanier, for she is described in practically the same words as in the Sonnets. We have already noted other characters from the actual background.

From the Sonnets we learn that William was reading Chaucer, in a new edition recently out, and, from the Knight's Tale, was minded to write a 'midsummer story'. This became the enchanting fairy-play, *A Midsummer Night's Dream*. This was amended, however, for a private production to grace the marriage of Southampton's mother with Sir Thomas Heneage, Vice-Chamberlain to Hunsdon as Lord Chamberlain. The distinguished elderly couple are the stately Duke and his bride in the play; but the young people who grace the proceedings come in, not from midsummer frolics, but from Maying on May Day. The Countess and Heneage, widow and widower, were married on 2 May 1594. *QED*.

The wedding was a private ceremony at which the Queen was *not* present. There is a hint that she was not best pleased with Heneage that spring. She never liked her favourites marrying, and here the besotted old fellow was marrying a Catholic too. Social sense should have told commentators that Shakespeare would never have greeted the Virgin Queen with lines against a 'virgin withering on a thorn'. But it never did: they listed all the noble marriages in the 1590s, as if any old marriage equalled any other, some of them missing this specific event in the Southampton circle. No social sense, no perception in the commentators.

II. The Southampton Circle

That autumn there took place a shocking event which might have led Southampton into serious trouble. The leading family in the next county, not far from Titchfield, were the Danvers brothers who pursued a prolonged feud with the Long family. The handsome younger brother, Henry, was a particular friend of Southampton, probably boy-friend, for he saved his charms and his money, made a fortune and entered the peerage. He also founded the Physic Garden at Oxford. The Danvers' mother was of an Italianate temperament and drove the feud on; a serving man was killed. On Justices' day, 4 October 1594, the brothers with their following entered the house at Corsham, where the Long faction were at meat. In the altercation that followed Henry Danvers shot at the heir of the Longs and killed him.

The brothers then fled to Titchfield for the Earl to conceal them, who put them up at a lodge in the park and fed them until they could make their getaway to France. This they successfully did, to lend their swords to the service of Henry of Navarre. The sheriff's posse in pursuit at the ferry over the Itchen was barracked by one John Florio. This was the Earl's Italian tutor, who served him for some years, and eventually won fame for

59

his Italian Dictionary. He too made a brief appearance in the circle in *Love's Labour's Lost*.

This gave William his cue for his next play. He knew Arthur Brooks's play, *Romeus and Juliet*, and speedily wrote his lyrical tragedy, *Romeo and Juliet*, a drama of love in the setting of a family feud. The setting was Italian – Shakespeare was becoming familiarised with Italy, if vicariously, what with Emilia and Florio, both Jewish in part. In the play there are touches of Marlowe in the character of Mercutio, with his preference for male friends rather than women and his dangerous partiality for affrays.

The more one knows of the facts behind these works the more one realises that all these people in that circle knew each other, and come alive to us.

At the very same time Southampton was in serious financial trouble. He had broken his word with his guardian, Lord Burghley, that he would marry the great minister's granddaughter. On reaching his full majority, 6 October 1594, he still refused to honour his promise. The Lord Treasurer was in no mood to put up with such an insult, and swiped him an enormous fine. Henceforth he found himself in considerable financial difficulties. With his devotion to Essex, he involved himself in opposition to the powerful Cecils. The Queen was not amused.

II. The Southampton Circle

When *Venus and Adonis* appeared, with Southampton as the reluctant Adonis, his poet furnished it with a Latin epigraph to challenge university wits at their own game:

Vilia miretur vulgus: mihi flavus Apollo
pocula Castalia plena ministret aqua.

'Let the mob admire what is base, to me let Apollo minister cups of pure water from Castalian springs.' He was still sensitive to the criticism he had received: 'I know not how I shall offend in dedicating my unpolished lines to your Lordship, nor how the world will censure me.' However, he 'vowed to take advantage of all idle hours [!] till I have honoured you with some graver labour.'

This took the form, now in 1594, of *The Rape of Lucrece*, certainly a graver, a sombre poem, full of guilt, violence and remorse. A tragedy, as against the naughty, high-spirited comedy of its predecessor: he could turn his hand to both. Gratitude for the young patron's support, tried in the crucible, shines forth: 'the love I dedicate to your Lordship is without end. What I have done is yours, what I have to do is yours, being part in all I have, devoted yours.' It was not only 'duty' that spoke thus, there was love that had survived two challenges to it in those three years since first 'thyself thou gav'st, thy own worth then not knowing, or me to whom thou gav'st it.'

However, he knew his own value, whatever the deference due, whatever the unkindnesses that had passed in such a long and tried relationship – 'if you were by my unkindness shaken, as I by yours.' He thought it better to be what he was than to live in others' 'false adulterate eyes', spying on his frailties though no better than himself. 'No: *I am that I am*' – and they can reckon up their own abuses. A later play, turning on the question of sex, innocence against guilt, how to measure one against the other in the inevitable mixture in which men and women are caught, has a most revealing matured reflection:

> They say men are moulded out of faults
> And, for the most part, become much more the better
> For being a little bad.

Evidently, always candid, that was what he really thought. Did his wife, the *hausfrau* at Stratford, think so too? – Silence – though we are told that, for all his work, his busyness in London, attendance on his patron, writing, acting, touring, he made time to go home to Stratford once a year, in summer.

Meanwhile his double, feverish life was far more

stimulating to the imagination. The scandal of his life would have referred to his affair with Emilia, which would have been known beyond their circle.

It was a tempestuous, unsatisfying affair, for though he was infatuated, Emilia certainly was not. For one thing, he was a good deal older, already balding and in the sere and yellow leaf, according to his candid self in the Sonnets. Moreover, he was only an actor, with no money and a family to support. With her high ideas, and herself perpetually dissatisfied with her lot, she spoke demeaningly of him, he complained, to their acquaintance. She looked down on him, as she looked down on her husband – from the conspicuous situation she had enjoyed – though this was in her nature too. Talented, educated, ambitious, it was maddening that she was a nobody now to the Court ladies she had known, some of whom could hardly write.

It was indeed a harassing affair, sometimes she was agreeable and willing, sometimes disagreeable and more willing to try others – she had to look out, fend for herself.

> Tell me thou lov'st elsewhere, but in my sight,
> Dear heart, forbear to glance thine eye aside

It was all humiliating for him, but he could not help

himself, though as usual he had no illusions. Both were adulterous, 'in act thy bed-vow broke'. So was his, and 'with mine compare thou thine own state'; she had sealed false bonds of love as oft as his, 'robbed others' beds' revenues of their rents.' He knew that she lied to him, and he accepted it

> That she might think me some untutored youth
> Unlearnèd in the world's false subtleties.

He recognised the falsehood on both sides. Why should his eyes, when he looked at her, think that she was his, when his heart knew that she was 'the wide world's commonplace'? She was known to be promiscuous, no unknown figure.

He acknowledged that his love was a sin, but nonetheless a fever:

> Past cure I am, now reason is past care,
> And frantic-mad with evermore unrest.

There were ups-and-downs in the relationship; sometimes she would say that she was his and make promises, then break them and aver that she hated him. He called her both tyrannous and contemptuous; no doubt she had the upper hand, for she had not that need which a highly sexed male had of her:

II. The Southampton Circle

The expense of spirit in a waste of shame
Is lust in action.

Then, on his side, 'thou know'st I am forsworn': on her side, 'thou art twice forsworn' in breaking vows to him as well as to her husband, whom she looked down on too, though he gave his name to the child she had by Henry, Lord Hunsdon: Henry Lanier. A couplet in the play, *The Two Gentlemen of Verona*, which uses up some of this experience, is revealing: there was a curse on love, 'when women cannot love when they're beloved.' We may sympathise with *her* too in her situation.

Still, whence had she this influence over him when all the time he saw their situation with utter clarity, worshipping her very defects, her becoming of things ill, putting a charm on them:

O from what power hast thou this powerful might
To make me give the lie to my true sight?

He saw through it all, at the same time as he was in thrall, no illusions: that is what makes the affair so authentic, at the same time as both parties were so exceptional. For, a few years later, we learn from her dealings with the astrologer Forman and the remarkable poem she wrote, *Salve Deus Rex Judaeorum*, Hail God King of the Jews, that she was psychic.

It was no ordinary young woman who infatuated this exceptional man. That in itself is convincing, however large the allowance we make for a highly imaginative poet, with whom things are apt to go to the head, and with a greater capacity for suffering, all too conscious of it. Such an affair could have no happy outcome – except in literature, where he used everything that came his way. It was the lady – if a questionable one – who ended it and gave him his dismissal.

He went to Bath for 'cure of love's disease', he says. At that time people went there for treatment of venereal infection, which was rife in contemporary London. Hunsdon's son, who succeeded him, after a brief interval, as Lord Chamberlain, was severely poxed:

> Fool hath he ever been
> With his Joan Silverpin,
> She makes his cockcomb thin
> And quake in every limb.

This last is borne out by his quaking signature.

> Quicksilver is in his head, etc.

That means the mercury treatment for syphilis.

Robert Cecil had it – according to his friend Ralegh – went to Bath and died on the way home. Peele the playwright had it. Another, Will Davenant – was he Will Shakespeare's boy? – lost his nose through a bad dose of pox from a 'black wench in Westminster' (this means a dark woman, not a black).

The poet describes his two loves, 'of comfort and despair', with complete clarity: one innocent and happy with 'a man right fair', as yet pure and untouched by women, the other with a woman 'coloured ill', bent on corrupting him. 'Suspect I may', though he could not 'directly tell', but 'I guess one angel in another's hell.' He remained worried, 'till my bad angel fire my good one out.' That sonnet is full of the word 'hell', which meant then, as with some today, the vagina, what Chaucer refers to as 'queynt'.

The outcome was *The Two Gentlemen of Verona*, entirely autobiographical in inspiration, given an Italian flavouring. Two friends are rivals for the same woman. The more volatile one betrays his steadier friend, who in the upshot makes way and in the play's *dénouement* resigns the lady to him on his repentance. All literary critics have condemned this as a hashed-up, improbable ending. It is precisely what happened between the poet and his patron. No wonder there was no other source for the play, though it has never occurred to the imperceptive to wonder why.

With the plague over in 1594, the actor was able to resume touring – he describes himself jogging on his nag along the roads. He is more away from London and apologises for absence from his patron: the earlier close relationship when Southampton was but a youth is loosening. The aspiring actor once and again expresses his resentment at being reduced to the profession, that fortune had not better provided for his life than 'public means which public manners breeds'.

He had gone here and there and 'made myself a motley to the view, sold cheap what is most dear' – his 'own thoughts'. No less wounding was it that his very name 'receives a brand' – revealing of the inner man again, for he feared that his nature might be 'subdued to what it works in'. How searching, how clinical a thought! Was it to happen?

At least security was at hand – at last – and in the lamented profession. Plague over, under the leadership of the Burbages, who were Hunsdon's Men, a select Company came together under his patronage and took their title from him, the Lord Chamberlain's Men.

II. The Southampton Circle

Southampton came up trumps and provided a handsome sum for his indigent poet to become not only a member of the Company but a leading sharer in its takings, along with the Burbages. Hitherto the leading Company had been the Lord Admiral's, for whom Marlowe had written his plays, with Edward Alleyn as its star, who shortly retired. Now the field was open for the Chamberlain's Company to take the premier place. William Shakespeare was its pivot – actor, producer, prolific playwright. Security at long last, he was to spend the rest of his life in the theatre, after all. Now he was a man of thirty, more than half of his life was over – and how much in it he had been through!

In bidding farewell to his patron, who had seen him through, he properly referred to him as 'the child of state', as he was, after all, a peer of the realm. The relationship had not been an external one, 'honouring' a Lord: he had observed all that in others, 'pitiful thrivers' he called them, rather superciliously, for they had their way to make too. So much had passed between those two.

There was the introduction of an ambitious provincial to cultivated aristocratic society, meeting with the great and grand, if not wholly good. His maturing sophistication has been observed in the images of the writer, even in his senses of smell and touch and sight.

69

In that society he found his true nature, what it cried out for, and for a writer, best of all – inspiration.

In the last of the Southampton Sonnets, that unique patronage sequence, he affirms that the relationship had been that of heart – still 'let me be obsequious in thy heart, poor but *free*'! And he ends with a claim to equality there – nothing else 'but mutual render, only me for thee.'

In the end it is a magnificent affirmation.

III

Theatre

I DO NOT PROPOSE to traverse the Plays in this book, merely keep an eye open for what is personal, what he says about himself, his acquaintance, interests, ambience. Of course his personality is obvious, in a sense, throughout, for no dramatist was ever so autobiographical. All critics have missed that. Occasionally there is a direct description of a contemporary event, or a topical reference which an historian can elucidate – as in the Sonnets, and that settles their dating, 1591/2, 1592, 1593, 1594/5. These occupy the most decisive period of his life, the essential experience, Southampton, Emilia, Greene and Marlowe. We should like to know more of what happened between him and those fellow writers ahead of him at the time of their early deaths. He was luckier – as things turned out, no writer more so. Never give up hope, never give in!

The sensation of the year 1594 was the trial and execution of Lopez, a Portuguese Jew who was the Queen's physician. He had been unwise enough to act as a double-agent for Spain and was accused of intending to poison her. She did not believe him guilty, but Essex gave lead to the outbreak of mob anti-Semitism which brought the poor doctor to the scaffold. All this led to the revival of Marlowe's play, *The Jew of Malta*, written for the Admiral's Company, now played again no fewer than fifteen times.

It was natural that Shakespeare's company, and their playwright, would want to go one better – as he did with *The Merchant of Venice*. Marlowe's play on the Jewish theme gave the starting point, but what a contrast! With this work Shakespeare indubitably went beyond his former rival. Against the brutal realism and knockabout farce of Marlowe's play, Shakespeare's is full of sentiment and sympathy. The opening theme is that of the loving friendship between Antonio, the Merchant, and Bassanio.

But the dominant interest centres upon Shylock the Jew, who is cheated of his expectations in the end. And this playwright moves on to a higher plane than the mob's: 'Hath not a Jew eyes? Hath not a Jew hands, organs, senses, affections, passions?... If you prick us, do we not bleed? If you poison us, do we not die?' I find that my sympathies are with Shylock.

Our particular interest is to observe how *close* Shakespeare was to this theme, and what a pointer is the name Bassanio. The Bassanos, the musical family to which Emilia belonged, were often called Bassani in London. They were Jewish, as was Southampton's tutor, Florio. The dramatist knew well what he was writing about.

Do we detect a rueful personal note, at the end of his agitated affair with Emilia – 'all things that are are with more spirit chased than enjoyed?' Again there is a mature philosophic scepticism regarding religious dogmatism in the observation: 'in religion what damned error but some sober brow will approve it with a text?'

The new Chamberlain's Company played at the Burbages' Theatre and Curtain: most of them would be familiar. The figures among them best known to the public were Richard Burbage, Shakespeare and Will Kemp, the comic star. Shakespeare created a splendid part for Burbage in Richard III, and the play became his most popular piece, holding the stage from that day to this. Richard's last line, 'A horse! a horse – my kingdom for a horse!' echoed through the centuries. Even years later the guide at Bosworth Field, instead of naming King Richard, 'he Burbage cried'.

The tale went round London that a young woman who fell for Burbage in the part gave an assignation to 'Richard' for that night. Shakespeare overheard it and forestalled him. When the message arrived that Richard III was at the door, the reply came that William the Conqueror was before him. *Ben trovato* – it was just the kind of thing that happened at the theatre, as we read in Forman's Case Books, and it gives us a glimpse of the playwright's reputation with people at large.

We find a reflection of grander associations in *Richard II*. Southampton was the leading follower of the Earl of Essex, the Queen's prime favourite in the early nineties, and also the favourite with the populace – an ambivalent role to play. This is noted, in the character of Bolingbroke – his 'courtship of the common people', doffing his hat to them, what reverence thrown away 'on slaves, wooing poor craftsmen with the craft of smiles'.

The dramatist himself made no such concession to the populace. From the beginning, with *Henry VI*, to the end they are unstable, unreliable,

> An habitation giddy and unsure
> Hath he that buildeth on the vulgar heart.

They will follow anybody who takes them in – a Wat Tyler or a Tom Paine, Hitler or Mussolini, or Stanley Baldwin. As that great democrat Franklin Roosevelt said, but not out loud: 'The public never understands.'

At that time it was Essex making up to them, increasingly to the Queen's distrust, as the critical time of the Succession approached. It is very interesting – though it has never been done – to watch the development of Shakespeare's views of the people's favourite, Southampton's leader. One can watch the change from earlier admiration to growing doubt and eventual mistrust. The dramatist had a view from the stalls of how things were at Court, from increasing performances there too. No wonder he makes a wonderful register of the time, as he came to recognise by the appearance of *Hamlet*. He saw through everybody and everything, with no illusions.

Shortly he came to live in Bishopsgate, where he was assessed for tax, now beginning to prosper, at a middling rate. There was the grand mansion, Crosby Place, to remind him that there Richard III had planned the strategy of his usurpation. A neighbour here was Thomas Morley, the delightful composer who set the song, 'It was a lover and his lass' to music, and perhaps 'O mistress mine'. Of all the playwrights

Shakespeare was the most responsive to music, evidently the most sensitive, from what he wrote about it. And we should note that it was from the time of his initiation in the Southampton circle that he made the most use of it.

It was while writing *King John* that he received a bad blow: his little boy, Hamnet, died at Stratford in August 1596, aged eleven. And we find the touching lines:

> Grief fills the room up of my absent child,
> Lies in his bed, walks up and down with me
> Puts on his pretty looks, repeats his words
> Remembers me of all his gracious parts,
> Stuffs out his vacant garments with his form,

It brings the boy visibly home to us, as so often with Shakespeare. And then, there was the belief

> That we shall see and know our friends in heaven:
> If that be true, I shall see my boy again.

He could not be certain; he had no dogmatic belief, but was content to rest his hope conformably with the beliefs of the time, not question them intellectually as Marlowe had done.

His thinking was largely in visual images, along with reflections on them. In this same play we have a vivid depiction of a blacksmith, hammer in hand, leaving his iron to cool on his anvil, to listen with open mouth to a gossipy tailor with shears and measure in hand. The tailor was in such a hurry to impart his improbable news of a French landing in Kent that he had thrust his slippers on wrong feet. What an eye! The scene closes with another 'unwashed artificer' butting in.

Here it is the gentleman of Henley Street speaking, and we happen to know that, round the corner, there was a blacksmith, one Hornsby. Since the player went home each summer, likely enough he was there that sad August when his boy died.

Reading Holinshed for subjects for these plays from English history yielded rich returns. They reached their summit in the next few years with the two parts of *King Henry IV* and the creation of his grandest comic character, Sir John Falstaff. Still, Warwickshire and Gloucestershire, particularly the Cotswolds, are in evidence in all. Sir John will not march his mouldy recruits through the cathedral city of Coventry, 'that's flat: there's but a shirt and a half in all my company – and the shirt stolen from my host at St Albans, or the red-nose innkeeper at Daventry. No eye hath seen such scarecrows.' They make good fun when they are reviewed and reckoned up.

Should a serving fellow's wages be stopped for 'the sack he lost the other day at Hinckley Fair'? There's a local dispute between Clement Perks of 'the Hill' and William Visor of Wincot – and we know too that there were Visors about, a local name he knew. 'How does your fallow greyhound, sir? I hear he was outrun on Cotsall.' (Cotswold.) 'What the devil are you doing in Warwickshire, when you should be well on the way to Shrewsbury?' 'You Banbury cheese!' Or perhaps, 'by'r Lady, 'a be but goodman Puff of Barston.' That is Barcheston, where the famous Sheldon tapestries were woven. Plenty of sport, and other activities, are going on in all that countryside.

London is much more to the fore now, not only the grandeur of the Court, familiar from frequent performances, the crises of historic monarchy, the well-drawn personalities of kings and courtiers.

The Court itself peregrinated from Whitehall, where it always was for Christmas time, to Greenwich and back, up the Thames, the highway of those centuries, to Hampton Court and on to Windsor. The playwright came to know these places familiarly, indeed dedicated a whole play to Windsor, *The Merry Wives*, at the command of the Queen, who wanted to see Sir John Falstaff again, in love. Tradition says that the farce was put together in a fortnight – convincingly enough, for it is mostly in easy prose with a personal tribute to her at the end.

London – especially the City – where Shakespeare was a lodger, for home was at Stratford, is much to the fore in the plays on Henry IV and Henry V. In these years he lodged for a time in little Silver Street, in the house of the Huguenot Mountjoys. We have a depiction of the house in a map of the time, twin gables and a shop pentice in front, for they were wig-makers – a theme which appears in his work, making use of everything (as poor Greene foresaw he would). The menfolk of the establishment were not very respectable, but in the documents the lodger is referred to deferentially as 'Master' Shakespeare. For it fell to him to perform the betrothal of the daughter of the house to the French apprentice, Bellot.

Master Shakespeare was on terms of confidence with Madame Montjoie. For the scenes in French in *Henry V* we need look no further. He had only to go down the street from here to Cheapside and St Paul's church-yard, where the publishers conveniently had their bookstalls. One block east and he was in the parish where lived his Fellows in the Company, Heming and Condell, to whom *we* owe so much for publishing his Plays after his death, and to whom he left remembrances in his will.

Relations with Stratford continued to be active. New Place, the fine gabled house he bought, needed repair and fitting up, for a load of stone left over was sold to the town. And, we find, 'when we mean to build we first survey the plot, then must we rate the cost, which if we find outweighs ability' … well, we can sell a load of stone – as later we find him selling a load of malt stored in the capacious house. Since that neighbour did not pay up he was taken to court; the cash was duly collected. Then a cottage with barn and garden was bought on the other side of the lane down from the Gild Chapel.

Since he was evidently prospering now, so busy in London, fellow townsmen thought he might invest in land out at Shottery, where the Hathaways farmed; or possibly invest in the tithes in Stratford. 'We think it a fair mark for him to shoot at. It would advance him indeed, and do us much good.'

In the event he did better. He bought just over a hundred acres in Old Stratford, the valuable former College's land around the church – think of the value of it today! However, he was so hard at work in the theatre that it was left to brother Gilbert, the haberdasher, to take formal possession of it for him.

III. Theatre

Neighbour Quiney favoured investing in tithes. In London on the town's business he had a meeting with William, though busy with three performances at Court during the Christmas season, from Christmas Eve to Twelfth Night, with another in February, 1597-8.

On a second visit Quiney found himself short of cash and hoped to borrow £30, a large sum, from his 'Loving Countryman', i.e. fellow Warwickshireman. 'You shall friend me much in helping me out of all the debts I owe in London. You shall neither lose credit nor money by me, the Lord willing. And now but persuade yourself so, as I hope, and you shall not fear.' He did not get the money. The Quineys were not an entirely reliable family, and William was more careful with money than his father had been – he had learned from hard experience over a good many years.

In the event he landed his biggest purchase, one half of the tithes of Welcombe and other country parishes around Stratford. This set him up as the independent country gentleman he had always meant to be in fact, as he thought himself all along.

The evocative *Henry IV* plays are full of memorable characters, King and Prince Hal, Falstaff and his miscreant thieving crew, his whore Doll Tearsheet and Mistress Quickly, Justice Shallow of Gloucester-shire senilely remembering London days. 'I was once of Clement's Inn, there was I and little John Doit of Staffordshire and Will Squeal a Cotswold man ... O, Sir John, do you remember how we lay all night in the windmill in St George's Fields?...'

People may not realise that in Falstaff there is more of his creator than his ready bubbling wit – which is all Shakespeare's. What did Falstaff think of fighting fools killing each other – all, *they* think, for Honour? Falstaff does not. 'What is Honour? A word. Can Honour set to a leg? No. Or an arm? No. Honour hath no skill in surgery then? No. What is that word Honour? Air. Who hath it? He that died o' Wednesday. Doth he feel it? No. Doth he hear it? No. It is insensible then? Yea, to the dead. But it will not live with the living? No. Therefore I'll none of it. Honour is a mere scutcheon.'

Does this represent what his creator thought? – the most prudent, tactful and courteous man of all the theatre folk. We know that as a gentleman wearing a sword he did not use it – as Marlowe and Watson did who killed William Bradley, or Ben Jonson who killed fellow actor, Gilbert Spencer, or Day and Porter, one of whom killed the other.

As for Prince Hal careering around with Falstaff and his crew, answering him with no less wit, it is only in our time that we have learned that Henry V, of Agincourt – the hero king to the Elizabethans – had led a dissipated youth, and underwent a real conversion on succeeding to the throne. Shakespeare was so much closer to the memories of that time (as with Richard III), so that his portraits and rendering of history have their authenticity, as well as their insight and comprehension. Literary folk have been sentimentally shocked at Henry's dismissal of the old rogue on becoming King – he had to be got rid of. It was good of Elizabeth I to have him revived for us.

Actors were as mobile as courtiers and knew their London well. The early school play, *The Comedy of Errors*, was based on Plautus, and the site of the Theatre and Curtain is described. It was formerly Holywell Priory, and in the vale were the gibbets where hangings took place – the land had come to the Rutland family at the Reformation. The play was performed in the Christmas season of 1594 both at Court and in the young lawyers' Revels at Gray's Inn. *Twelfth Night* was performed at Court and in the Middle Temple Hall, as well as regularly in the Company's repertory. 'Meet me tomorrow at the Temple Hall.'

A frequent place of meeting was the long nave of Old St Paul's, like a street or concourse for business, exchange of news, ragamuffins, street walkers, every common sort. 'He's gone into Smithfield to buy your worship a horse. – I bought him in Paul's.' 'This oily rascal is known as well as Paul's.' Moorfields and St George's Fields were where the City's militia mustered and citizens took the air. Or on the Thames, crowded with watermen and wherries, the taxis of the time. Shooting the arches under London Bridge was an expert's job, apt to be dangerous, according to the tide. 'Away! You'll lose the tide if you tarry any longer.' The Thames swans are often noted, as those at Stratford were in the early plays – and Ben Jonson was to hail him as 'the Swan of Avon'.

In 1598 Southampton became trapped, in the usual way: he got a lady pregnant. Though Elizabeth Vernon was a maid-of-honour to the Queen, as usual he did not want to marry and left her vulnerable, in doubt. He flung off out of the way to France, where in Paris he lost large sums at tennis – this would be the real (royal) tennis of the time. Summoned home, the Queen sent him to the Fleet to cool his heels. The dowerless young lady was Essex's cousin, and at the last moment he made the Earl make her his Countess in a secret marriage. She always remained in love with her wayward volatile man, still something of an adolescent.

In this year 1598 broke out the most dangerous rebellion in Ulster, led by the remarkable, politic O'Neil. Essex claimed the leadership of the large army sent to recover the position. The people's hero was given a grand send-off from the City. 'Behold, how London doth pour out her citizens, the mayor and all his brethren, the plebeians swarming at their heels.' Next year, the country waited for results, – 'were now the General of our gracious Empress, as in good time he may', subdue rebellion and return to popular applause again.

Essex did nothing of the sort. Instead of tackling Ulster while his forces were fresh, he wasted time on footling expeditions about the country, arguing the toss with the government at home which had exhausted resources to equip him. The Queen was furious and sent him bitter reproaches of a royal eloquence. He had already offended by appointing Southampton as General of Horse. On him she added a tart reminder: 'Yea, such a one was – were he not lately fastened to yourself by an accident, wherein for our usage of ours we deserve thanks [he had been confined but briefly] – you would have used many of your old lively arguments against him for any ability of commandment.' There was the Queen's opinion of Southampton. Actually he was never wanting in courage and performed a hardy exploit in the field, slightly wounded. Never mind: he was down-graded, cashiered.

All this added to Essex's dissatisfaction and complaints at failure. Instead of bringing 'rebellion broached on his sword', he made a hurried truce with O'Neil and entered into dangerous discussion with him as to what should happen when the Queen died. He evidently meant to control the succession of James of Scotland.

That question was in everybody's mind at the time. *Hamlet* was being written. Succession to the throne of Denmark is the crux of the play – sufficiently removed in place and time for safety. We find a reflection of Essex in this context:

> The courtier's, soldier's, scholar's, eye, tongue, sword
> The expectancy and rose of the fair state,
> The glass of fashion and the mould of form,
> The observed of all observers.

He was indeed being observed, people not certain what he would do. One sharp pair of eyes saw, with some distrust, 'favourites, made proud by princes,

advance their pride against the power that bred it.'
This was exactly the case now between Elizabeth I
and Essex, when he rushed back home having ac-
complished nothing, to meet disgrace. Something
more of Essex's hesitation, havering and hovering,
unable to make up his mind on what course to take,
may also be reflected in the Prince of Denmark.
Burghley was certainly Polonius in the play; it was
now safe to caricature him, for he had died in 1598,
the prosy, omniscient minister, with his Precepts
warning his son against the cult of popularity. The
all-powerful Cecils were not popular and were tar-
gets for the irresponsibles of the Essex-Southampton
group, to which Shakespeare was personally indebted – those were his friends. Still, Sir Robert Cecil
resorted to a play of Shakespeare's when he wanted
an entertainment for *his* friends at his private house.

Eventually Essex fell for open rebellion, pushed on by
Southampton – and that was fatal. The night before the
outbreak in the City, some of Essex's followers got
Chamberlain's Men to put on *Richard II*, to remind
people that monarchs could be deposed. The Queen
was angered by this too – 'am I not Richard II?'; but the
players were not sued, for they were not responsible.
Essex was executed, Southampton was condemned to
death, sent to the Tower, his sentence suspended, held

over his head. He made a favourable impression at his trial, still looking youthful. His mother wrote to Cecil for mercy, pleading that her son's inability to win the Queen's favour was the cause of his going astray. He was not reprieved, but remained in the Tower, until James I on his safe accession freed him. We have a portrait of him there – he was apparently unrepentant – long hair flowing, a book before him, attended by his cat, who looks more knowing than the Earl.

In 1599 took place a great transformation in the theatre. The Burbages transferred the timbers from their old playing house north of the City to the South Bank of the Thames and built a grand new theatre, the Globe. Much bigger, with galleries around and a big apron stage jutting out into the audience, so that productions had a three-dimensional effect, unlike the modern picture stage. The audience was much more involved in the action, therefore showed greater excitement in response to the rhetoric – the Elizabethans had a regular ritual of gestures to point up emotional expression. Everything was more exciting and, with no changes of scene and no intermissions, the speed and cumulative effect must have been electrifying.

III. Theatre

Henry V was ready in time for the opening of the Globe. We have a salute to it in the Prologue. It was in construction round – 'so may we cram within this wooden O the very casques of Agincourt? Can this cockpit hold the vast fields of France?' Then, with the regular courtesy that was characteristic of him, addressing them all as gentlefolk, asking pardon for the flat unraised spirits that have dared to bring forth these great events on this unworthy scaffold.

Hence the very different character of this play from *Henry IV*: no Falstaff, far fewer comic episodes, more pageantry and action, with a Chorus between each act to describe historic events. He most likely played the part of Chorus, for in the Epilogue he pleads that the 'bending author' has pursued the story with 'rough, unable pen'. Rough, unable pen, indeed! It is like his self-deprecation in the Sonnets, with Marlowe as the 'worthier pen'. It gives us the opportunity to rejoin that, in spite of his regret at having to take to acting for a living, the challenge of the theatre, the drama called forth his finest poetry.

Tributes to him now flowed fast and from all sides, in his case exceptionally as both poet and playwright.

The young poet Barnfield regarded himself as his disciple:

> And Shakespeare, thou whose honey-flowing vein,
> Whose *Venus* and whose *Lucrece* sweet and chaste
> Thy name in Fame's immortal book have placed.

His poetry seems to have been particularly admired at Cambridge – by John Weever, and his tutor Clovell. Grumpy Gabriel Harvey, friend of Spenser, said that *Venus and Adonis* was most popular – it went into more editions – but that the graver sort took to *The Rape of Lucrece*. From remote Cornwall Richard Carew compared him with Catullus. Even the Jesuit martyr, Southwell, wrote:

> Still finest wits are stilling [distilling] Venus' rose.

Of his 'sugared sonnets' a few circulated among his private friends.

There was agreement in applying the word honeyed to his work: he was 'sweet' Shakespeare, above all the poet of love, the English Ovid – who was indeed his own favourite. We are ourselves reminded today – by Santayana – of the 'honey by which great poets have sweetened words'. When Francis Meres summed up contemporary writers in 1598, Shakespeare is the only one who appears in both categories, and for the stage in both comedy and tragedy, the English Plautus and Seneca. Tribute is paid to him too among those who have enlarged and enriched the language. The language itself was in a most pregnant condition, taking in words in force to express the bounding, expanding time, new experiences notably overseas, a New World, India, the Far East. He was foremost in expanding our vocabulary – to twice that used in ordinary speech – all to express the life, the excitement, the wonder of the age.

The year 1598 had seen the publication at last of Marlowe's *Hero and Leander*, completed by the less inspired, workmanlike George Chapman. This brought to the surface the memory of his unhappy former rival; in the play written at the time there are three or four references to Marlowe and the poem he had not completed – 'all air and fire', Drayton said of him – at the time he died.

Another character to cross Shakespeare's path, and come into our view, was the swaggering, rumbustious, awkward customer, Ben Jonson, eight years his junior. A less good actor, he had something new to contribute to the stage, a critical, satirical vein not natural to his senior. Shakespeare took him under his wing, recruited him to the Chamberlain's Men and himself acted in Ben's first, masterly *Everyman in his Humour.*

Too restless to remain with them long, Ben moved on to work with the Boys' Companies who performed at the little theatre in Blackfriars. They specialised in topical satire, which became the fashion for a time, competing with and challenging the Men's Companies. This led to a regular rumpus and rows, other playwrights like Marston and Dekker weighing in, and much rudeness on both sides – though it must have been good for business.

Shakespeare was writing *Hamlet* at the time and wasted none on controversy. All he said in that play, which tells us so much of what he thought about the stage and acting, was this: 'There has been much to do on both sides, much throwing about of brains.' As for the boys, the 'little eye-asses' – a bawdy innuendo for people in the audience who knew well what was said about the boys and the men actors, even about Ben (never about William, with him it was always about women) – 'They are now the fashion', so popular that they 'berattle the common stages, as they call them.' Their topical plays did indeed appeal to the more select audience at Blackfriars. 'Do the boys carry it away?' What will happen to them when their voices break and they can no longer sing? Their writers are doing them a wrong, for then they may be reduced to acting on the common stages, 'if their means are no better'. We note a touch of the old resentment of years before at having to earn his living by public means, 'which public manners breeds'. In notorious fact it had not done so in his case, the gentleman of the theatre.

Called upon by the Queen to entertain her in her declining years, he responded speedily with a merry farce placed at Windsor, where Sir John Falstaff is made a fool of by the good bourgeois wives of the town. At the Castle let the fairies pinch the maids blue if they neglect the fires and hearths, for

> Our radiant Queen hates sluts and sluttery.

May the Castle stand till doomsday in good state,

> Worthy the owner and the owner it.

At Stratford his father died in 1601, his mother, Mary Arden, seven years later. On the eve of Lady Day, 24 March 1603 that formidable old lady, the Queen, died. A new age opened, for him and everybody.

In 1601 appeared a curious book, *Love's Martyr*, edited by one R. Chester. It was a collection of tributes to celebrate the married happiness of one of the Welsh Salusbury family, whose wife was one of the noble Stanleys. To this a bevy of playwrights contributed, Jonson, Chapman, Marston. By far the most remarkable poem was Shakespeare's, 'The Phoenix and the Turtle'. It is a strange poem, strangely beautiful and remote in a way – today one might say surrealist: in Elizabethan terms, emblematic.

Again strangely, this poem is more of a requiem:

> So they loved, as love in twain,
>   Had the essence but in one:
>   Two distinct, division none,
> Number there in love was slain.

It concludes with an exquisite 'Threnos':

> Beauty, truth, and rarity,
> Grace in all simplicity,
> Here enclosed in cinders lie.

> Death is now the phoenix' nest,
> And the turtle's loyal breast
> To eternity doth rest.

III. Theatre

Leaving no posterity:
'Twas not their infirmity,
It was married chastity.

What a curious tribute, standing out among the rest! He had always been known as the foremost poet of love in that time, now he is celebrating the death of love. Yet it is characteristic, for he celebrates married love – which he had all along favoured, from the first Sonnets onwards.

But how remarkable to have produced this esoteric poem – an example of *la poésie pure* – not long after creating *Hamlet*'s world of imagination and the farce of *The Merry Wives*, and shortly before the bitter, satirical *Troilus and Cressida*! Poor Robert Greene's forecast was certainly fulfilled in the perfect 'Johannes Factotum' who in time would wipe the floor of all of them. As now again, in competing with the intellectual strain of younger poets – the likes of John Donne, whose uncongenial idiom he had remarked on in the Sonnets, never by name, of course.

IV

Jacobean

IN THE general euphoria of James I's quiet accession from Scotland, it was a new age for Shakespeare, and for Southampton too. He was released from the Tower, taken into favour, and given several offices and promotions. That December the Court was at Wilton, where the Chamberlain's Men played and Southampton was present. How much we should like to know what passed! The new King and Queen were avid to see all the new plays denied to them in the Calvinist amenities of Edinburgh. At a private performance James was able to see the old *Love's Labour's Lost* called up again by Southampton, for whom it had been originally written.

After the gloom of Knox and (worse) Melville's Edinburgh, the English stage offered immense relief and received even more marked royal favour. The Chamberlain's Men, as the premier Company, became the King's Men, its leading figures promoted Grooms of the Royal Bedchamber. Their fee for a performance at Court was doubled from what the appreciative, but more frugal, Elizabeth had allowed. The Admiral's

Men became Prince Henry's, Worcester's Men Queen Anne's.

People rushed to see the new monarch. James I was a timorous man who had had several frights from his uncivil subjects in Scotland. A clever man – with his intellectual interests, he was more like a don than a king – such a contrast with the late Queen, her glittering jewelled appearances and infallible stagey gifts. The Elizabethan stage! – she had been its one and only actress. A proclamation was put forth, asking the multitude to restrain their enthusiasm.

The tactful dramatist, always ready to fall in with the wishes of government, commended this in a new play, *Measure for Measure.* He said that 'the general populace' might well be anxious to welcome a 'well-wished King', but crowding round him gave offence. 'I love the people' (did he?) but he didn't like to stage himself to their eyes for their applause.

All's Well That Ends Well takes its suggestion from Southampton's story, and recapitulates its leading features – Shakespeare making use, as so often, of what came his way, in books or experience, his own or of the time. Needs must – two plays a year to provide for his Company. What is the subject? A spoiled young Count will not marry the girl who is in love with him. His mother, a charming character – as Southampton's own mother was – favoured the marriage. So did his sovereign, in the play a king. Rather than enter upon marriage, the young Count flunks off abroad – as Southampton had done. In the play the Count performs a gallant exploit – as the young Earl had done in Ireland. But the Count can be got into the marriage-bed by a trick. It would be ungallant of us to regard Elizabeth Vernon's pregnancy as a trick, though in the event it got him – and the marriage turned out happily.

That family man, the actor-poet-playwright, had been in favour of marriage all along.

James I continued – what was expected of him – the royal rite of touching for the King's Evil, ancient anthropological mummery for curing sufferers from scrofula and various skin diseases. Shakespeare gives him credit for doing his unpleasant duty – we have a gruesome depiction of the deceased, 'the mere despair of surgery', whom of course he cures. This 'strange virtue' is carried on to succeeding monarchs. We know that the rite reached its peak with James's sainted grandson, Charles II, whose niece, Queen Anne, 'touched' Dr Johnson when a boy, with prayers, for his complaint. Surprisingly, this did not cure him, but it confirmed his Stuart sympathies.

On 5 November 1605 there broke upon London the sensation of the Gunpowder Plot, celebrated ever since as Guy Fawkes Day. A gang of young Catholic gentry, disappointed that James had not brought in the toleration they expected – as if that were possible – entered into a dangerous conspiracy to blow up King and Parliament at its opening. Ordinary Catholics were loyal, but those who were under the influence of the Machiavellian Jesuit, Parsons, were a different kettle of fish: he was a traitor, for he conspired by every means, and with Spanish aid, to overthrow the régime.[1]

The Jesuit Provincial, Garnet, had remained undisturbed until this thunderclap. But he had learned in confession that some conspiracy was afoot. He was brought to trial, when even the Catholic Northampton, a Howard, said that he could have informed someone in authority, i.e. himself, who could have put a stop to it. Garnet's defence was based on the Jesuit doctrine of equivocation: under duress one might equivocate. This made a most unpopular impression, and the popular dramatist took it up in the play. What was an equivocator? – 'One that could swear in both scales against either scale, who committed treason enough for God's sake.' What is a traitor? asks a boy. Why, one that swears on oath and then lies – he deserves hanging.

The plea of the seminary priests sent into England was that they came only for religion's sake. That was

---

1. For him *v.* 'Father Parsons the Jesuit', in my *Eminent Elizabethans*.

not true of Parsons and his followers, who had political aims; but even the aims of the unpolitical were to upset the religious settlement, the consensus arrived at under Elizabeth. The innocent were caught in the trap laid for them by the indoctrination of Father Parsons, as John Donne exposed it in his *Pseudo-Martyr*. Some of Donne's family had been victims. When his eyes were opened he regarded them as pseudo-martyrs, their sacrifice of their lives unnecessary. Shakespeare had seen that point years before, in a Sonnet of 1594, when he called them 'the fools of time, which die for goodness which have lived for crime.' They died for their religion, but their entry into the country contrary to its laws was a criminal offence with penalties that were well advertised.

The dramatist responded again to the popular mood with a play on a Scottish theme, *Macbeth*. The royal house was supposed to be descended from a legendary Banquo, to whom are attributed royalty of nature, dauntless temper, valour and wisdom. These could be transferred loyally to James, whose bearing was not very royal; he had wisdom of a sort, but was neither dauntless nor valorous. Banquo had not been a King, but it was prophesied that he would beget kings, even one who would unite the two kingdoms, his prime gift to the island of Britain. Moreover, his line would stretch

105

out to the crack of doom. Well, they are happily with us still in spite of everything.

James was duly gratified and, we learn, 'was pleased with his own hand to write an amiable letter to Master Shakespeare.' What makes this sound convincing is that the lost letter 'remained long in the hands of Sir William Davenant'. This in turn rather reinforces *his* connection with his godfather.

In the last unhappy months of Queen Elizabeth's reign Shakespeare wrote one of his most brilliant, and least popular plays, *Troilus and Cressida*. It has great intellectual interest, particularly for his views on society and political order, and was probably intended for private performance. Always something new – so many of the Plays represent a new step in his dramaturgy, an expansion of his art. This rather bitter play reflects acutely, eloquently, the queasy time in which it was written. It has several direct reflections on Essex, whose fate dominated it – the end of that career which began so promisingly and ended in disaster.

Here he is, as he was: 'possessed with greatness', pride impelling him to quarrels, not only with Cecil's government but with the Queen herself. 'Things small as nothing he makes important' – that had been his way, always pestering her for offices, promotions for his friends, forming a party to bring pressure, hoping to oust the government. 'He is so plaguy proud that the death-tokens of it cry "No recovery".' There was indeed none: Essex brought his fall upon himself. The close observer of these events saw that when such contenders for power fall, the love that leaned on them proved just as slippery: they slipped away, some went over to the government, as Francis Bacon did and notoriously took part in his former leader's trial.

Why is *Troilus and Cressida* – a wonderful play to the elect capable of appreciating it – so bitter and searing? For one thing it is a bitter experience to watch one's friends, one's group or party steering straight for the rocks – and Shakespeare's personal affiliations were all with the Essex-Southampton group, not with the Cecils and the Government on the other hand. It added to the stress when Shakespeare, always in favour of authority and order, and with a very clear head intellectually, saw that the government was right. This is apt to be searing, it tears a man in two, heart against brain.

The times themselves were out of joint, the war was going on and on – was there no end to it? *Hamlet* had had a severe reflection on the siege of Ostend for two or three years, thousands of men dying for 'a little patch of ground of no profit but the name.' The Trojan War, the background of the new play, had gone on and on – and what for? – all over a whore, the divisive Helen. Cressida was no better, passing easily from the arms of a Trojan to those of a Greek – just as Emilia Lanier had passed from one lover to another. The pimp Pandarus says the last word on womankind, as the scurrilous cynic Thersites does on men and their silly affairs. The play is one of utter disillusionment with love as well as war, the world of action. No wonder it has never been popular.

But it is full of words of wisdom, of salutary wisdom, with magnificent speeches given to the wise oracle, Ulysses. It is very remarkable that Shakespeare should have understood that there is 'a mystery in the soul of state', i.e. the body politic, the very nature of society. Few people ever understand it, certainly not those intellectuals, Marlowe and Ben Jonson. His understanding must be instinctive, and he had shown it all along. He went on to say that it should not be 'meddled' with, or worse would befall.

Disruption of the social order brought calamity. Society was based on proper organisation of degree, according to men's function in it. When this organisation is 'shaked', see what 'discord', what breakdown follows. We have had the advantage of being able to see the consequences in Communist Russia following upon

Revolution. He asks how could social arrangements hold together, communities, 'brotherhoods in cities', schools, commerce, exchange, agriculture, the running of estates, the land, right up to government and monarchy? Disruption and breakdown would ensue.

The consequences would be a mere power struggle, he diagnoses. Power, a universal appetite, would eat up everything; strength would prevail over the weak, no right or wrong, no justice or law, it would eventually consume itself. We have seen that happen in our time. Nine out of Lenin's Politburo, his cabinet of eleven, were eaten up by Stalin. Hitler killed off a number of his former comrades, the leaders of his SA troops. The French Revolution provided a similar lesson with the revolutionaries eating each other up in their power struggle.

Shakespeare was profoundly right in his diagnosis. We must interpose to say that Elizabethan England was a very successful society, as societies go: people abroad recognised it at the time, along with the exceptional success of its government. Shakespeare saw further – that the crust of social order is thin, civilisation brittle: once broken through, what dark forces open up beneath. And how difficult it is to reorganise a social order. Behold Russia today!

England too has had its severe lessons. In the time of

Shakespeare's grandfather there had been the murder-
ous bloodshed of the Wars of the Roses, which provided
the dramatist with so much material for his early plays,
and plenty to think about. In his daughter's time was to
come the worse experience of the Civil War, a pro-
founder shake-up to society, its re-establishment a
difficult job over years. The family at Stratford was
monarchist, and his daughter Susanna entertained
poor Queen Henrietta on her way to aid the embattled
Charles I.

How much more is observed in this searching play!
Men are like butterflies in summer: they follow the
sunshine of prosperous success, not rating honour for its
own sake but simply external honours, 'places, riches
and favour, prizes of accident as oft as merit.' On the
positive side – amid the disenchantment, cynicism, false
heroics held up to scorn – he tells us something that
reveals himself. No man is fully himself till 'he commu-
nicates his parts to others'. He was not unsociable,
certainly not a withdrawn observer. Still more revealing: a man hardly knows what he is capable of until his
gifts are extended, shaped up, in the applause of others.
We see that this would very much apply to a playwright,
less so to a poet.

One wonders why this brilliant but disturbing play

is not performed more often? Too near the bone, I suspect.

In 1606 came *King Lear*. Some people think this the summit of Shakespeare's achievement, when in fact there are several summits, in different ways. This play has an epic quality, with its vast spread – the elements themselves are brought in play, the old mad King exposed to them wandering in a storm over the heath.

With good 'box office' sense, Shakespeare was always alert to what was going on at the time. Curiously enough, something suggestive was happening to a courtier, Brian Annesley, whom he may have known as Master of the Harriers. A daughter with her husband tried to get the old man certified as a lunatic to get hold of his possessions. A younger daughter, Cordell, or Cordelia, endeavoured to protect him from the rapacious couple.

This girl shortly after married Sir William Harvey (Master W.H.), Southampton's young stepfather, after the death of the Countess. She left him all the goods and chattels at Southampton House – including, evidently, the manuscripts of the sonnets and 'A Lover's Complaint'. The more one digs *deeply* into these things – as few have done – the more they come together.

King Lear is a vast world in itself, so we do not expect many touches of the time. The atmosphere, however, is still that of disillusion, almost despair. Gloucester, a good man, is blinded by an evil one. 'Get thee glass eyes, and seem to see the things, thou dost not – like a scurvy politician.' In those days the word 'politician', perhaps the concept, bore a pejorative sense. 'A man may see how this world goes with no eyes.' Justice? There were frequent miscarriages of justice – and 'handy-dandy, which is the Justice, and which is the thief?' With his responsible point of view (unlike Marlowe) Shakespeare properly respected authority. Nevertheless he saw through the pretences of local jacks-in-office – 'a dog's obeyed in office'. A rascal of a beadle would lash a poor whore when, strip *him*, he'd like to use her services himself. No illusion anywhere is the word.

From touring he was fairly acquainted with Southern England, no sign of the North. 'Know'st the way to Dover?' At the end of August 1606 the King's Men were playing there. That he was among them may be inferred from his description of what is known today as Shakespeare's Cliff with, in those days, its samphire gatherers. 'How fearful and dizzy 'tis' to look down so

low, crows and choughs no larger than beetles. 'Half
way down hangs one that gathers samphire – dreadful
trade!' The fishermen on the beach look like mice, and
one can hardly hear the sea murmuring on the pebbles
from so high.

The play was performed at Court in the Christmas
season – hence written that autumn.

Next year, 1607, at Stratford elder daughter Susanna
was married to Dr John Hall, a Cambridge man
whose book of prescriptions has survived. From this
we watch him treating the gentry around the county,
also the poet Drayton, and we note a few more
medical observations in the Plays testifying to family
talks. In Southwark the youngest Shakespeare, Edmund, also an actor, died that bleak midwinter. He
was buried in the church, now Southwark Cathedral,
to the knell of the great bell. We may guess who paid
for that, for William had transferred his lodging to
the South Bank, following the Globe thither.

We know how popular his plays continued to be –
indeed he never lost the ear of the audience, as Ben
Jonson sometimes did.

> The cockpit, galleries, boxes are all full
> To hear Malvolio, that cross-gartered gull –

when people would not come to hear Jonson's *Sejanus* or *Catiline*. Again the 'multitude' were drawn to hear Brutus' speeches justifying Caesar's assassination and Mark Antony's more 'eloquent' defence of him 'showing his virtues'.

This year another Roman play followed, *Antony and Cleopatra*, based like *Julius Caesar* on North's translation of Plutarch's Lives. This volume belonged to Richard Field, who had taken over its publication from Vautrollier, and added matter subsequently. It was so ready to hand for his old friend that we find North's eloquent prose sometimes transferred recognisably in the plays. Then we remember how close blank verse is to the natural rhythms of English speech.

Ben criticised his senior for being insufficiently classical. But Shakespeare, by nature imaginatively romantic, had his own idea of classicism. *Julius Caesar* is an example: streamlined and rigorous, no comic distractions from the 'argument' (a favourite word). And *Coriolanus* is still more so, of classic structure and uncoloured regularity.

Antony and Cleopatra is totally different – we might call it a romantic masterpiece, full of golden glow, like a Roman sunset, or rich colouring like a Venetian Veronese. Our particular interest, as indeed everybody's, is in the character of Cleopatra, for she is unique

among Shakespeare's women. Agatha Christie, expert
in detection and a good Shakespearean, had the insight
that in drawing Cleopatra he was remembering some-
body. She is mercurial and temperamental,
up-and-down, using her sexual magnetism to keep a
hold on her man, treating him casually. She is tyranni-
cal – and the dark lady in the sonnets is described as
'tyrannous'. Cleopatra is a *donna mobile*, undependable,
she will let her lover down when it suits her. Above all
she is ambitious; the clue to her is that she was *alien:* this
is why the Romans hated her. Well, Emilia Bassano was
not only ambitious but half-alien: she had not an English but an Italianate character – perhaps her exoticism
was part of her appeal. Creative writers create out of
underlying experience, often subconsciously: there is
something of her character in Cressida, more in Cleopatra. As the philosophic Santayana enforces, 'Nature
is the moving ground of experience, and experience a
play of moral counterpoint or conscious crosslights
upon the surface of nature.'

Here is such a moral crosslight: in our ignorance we
often beg for what is harmful to us; this is often 'denied
to us for our own good – so we profit by losing of our
prayers.' For the rest, never had sheer poetry reached
greater heights: the heart turns over at hearing such
phrases: 'darkling stand the varying shore of the world',

115

or 'there is nothing left remarkable beneath the visiting moon.' The challenge of action, conflict, fate in drama brought out the deepest poetry. It must ere this have reconciled the poet in him to the 'public means' of its expression.

Though he owed his prosperity to the theatre, he remained one of the poetic confraternity, Barnfield's chosen four, with Spenser, Drayton, Daniel. The admirable Daniel, historian as well as poet, was closest in spirit to the most historically minded of playwrights. In revising his own play *Cleopatra* he made alterations reflecting Shakespeare's. Daniel was a friend of Philip Sidney's sister, who was engaged in publishing her dead brother's work. When Emilia came to publish her own long poem a few years later, *Salve Deus Rex Judaeorum*, it had an inset of *Antony and Cleopatra*, closer to Daniel rather than her long-estranged lover.[2]

Affairs in Stratford were not neglected. The gentleman of New Place was owed a debt by one Addenbrooks, who could not be found – so he put the fellow's surety through the Court and collected the money. In Court he noted the romantic name of

2. For this see my edition, *The Poems of Shakespeare's Dark Lady*.

Florizel – filed away for future use: he was a magpie for picking up tips, from everywhere and everyone.

Public affairs in the neighbourhood were disturbed with an agrarian rising over enclosure of arable and a severe dearth of corn that year, 1608. The trouble spread with peasants up in arms from the Midlands into Warwickshire. Some of his fields – he was now a landed gent – were threatened by removal of boundary ditches and fences overthrown; he was informed, but was away at the time. His neighbour, William Combe, reported the people's grievances to the government. The tumult quietened down, but the fact was that, with the Jacobean peace, the national unity achieved in the war against Spain, class conflict came to the fore. All this came into the next play, *Coriolanus*.

There could not be a greater contrast with the luscious ripeness of *Antony and Cleopatra*, written like *Romeo and Juliet* and *Othello* in the full flood of emotional inspiration. *Coriolanus* was based on a good deal of reading, its interest for us mainly political and social. This is brought home by the fact that, when produced in the Leftist Paris of the 1930s, it caused a riot, for it is uncompromisingly anti-democratic, harsher than before – as is its hero, Coriolanus, who will not submit to the humiliating demands of a popular vote. He hates the humbug of it – of which the late Stanley Baldwin

117

was a master in our own time. Some humbug is no doubt a necessary element in politics, but Coriolanus will not accept degrading concessions. Though he has saved the Roman Republic, he is thrown into exile by the people and goes over to the enemy.

Shakespeare had never nourished democratic illusions or respected popular political wisdom, from his caricature of Jack Cade's in *Henry VI*. And we realise now – as people did not earlier – that he had the sympathies of his middle- and upper-class audiences with him. Of course – *QED*. 'Care for us? They never cared for us yet!' Today there is a popular cliché about 'caring' government. In fact the Jacobean government did do something to relieve distress, distributing corn, in spite of its lack of resources and the difficulties of communication.

Some people were dissatisfied with peace, and preferred the activity and opportunities, the chances of war. Particularly the men of action. There is an incisive passage in *Troilus* about those who esteem nothing but action, regarding policy as cowardice. Activists despise 'the still and mental parts' that do the contriving and planning, weigh up the strength of opponents, and estimate their resources. They call this 'bed-work, mappery, closet war'. This had been the line of Essex and Ralegh, with their followings, against the brainwork, the political judgement of Burghley, Robert Cecil and the Queen, that insurmountable trio.

How could the complex issues of politics be 'concluded by the yea-and-no of general ignorance?' The 'real necessities' of the state and of society are neglected, nothing done to purpose. Those who stand out against the decline of standards and social breakdown are discounted: 'manhood called foolery when it stands against a falling fabric.' As usual there are specific observations as to how men behave in politics. Watch the 'slippery turns. Friends fast sworn, as twins unseparable, shall on a dissension of a doit break out to bitterest enmity.' Similarly foes, 'whose plots have broke their sleep', shall grow dear friends and join together to push their plans. 'Slippery' is the regular word he uses for the ways of the Court and politics.

V

Blackfriars Again

IN 1608 came a new development in the theatre world of increasing importance as time went on. The Burbages owned the property of the private theatre within the aristocratic precinct of Blackfriars, where the Hunsdons also had property. They had leased the theatre to one of the Boys' Companies, and now decided to take it back as a second playing house for the King's Men. Two or three helped with the money for the repurchase. The now very successful dramatist was one, so that he became a part owner of this theatre, one of half a dozen sharing the profits, which in time outgrew those of the Globe.

For Blackfriars was an upper-class theatre with a well-to-do audience, roofed-in and snug for winter performances, not open to the elements like the popular houses. The new conditions offered prospects for new effects: more intimate candle-lit scenes, more music, and the adaptation of the masques which were more and more fashionable at Court.

Blackfriars was fashionable, and offered a new challenge to the Master always ready to experiment. The plays he was to write for it included more music and made use of masques. A promising young couple, Beaumont and Fletcher, were recruited to write new kinds of plays suited to the more select audience and of more limited popular appeal. Their more experienced senior, familiar with all sides of theatrical life and flexibly minded as ever, had an appeal for both audiences, still more markedly for the Court. He did not lose hold on the Globe either – though the profits from Court and Blackfriars performances grew larger.

Again one observes his constant, and ready, response to the atmosphere and prominent features of the time. In 1607 at last a permanent colony was established in America at Jamestown. Widespread interest was aroused from 1609 when it received a new Charter and some hundreds of people subscribed to the venture, becoming Adventurers to Virginia (i.e. North America). Southampton, now a member of the government and a Protestant, a sadder and a wiser man, had taken an interest in American exploration while in the Tower. He now came to the fore, took a leading part in the Adventurers, and ended up at the head as Treasurer. One of the earliest Hundreds in Virginia was named for him, now Chickahominy Hundred.

These new developments are at once reflected in the Master's new plays. They are full of sea adventures and travels. They are also experimental. We do not know whether another hand was involved in *Pericles*, of which only an unsatisfactory text has come down to us, while *Timon of Athens* was never completed – perhaps understandably, with the new theatre developments and disturbed conditions in the printing trade. For in 1608 plague held up matters again. It used to be thought that Shakespeare took no interest in the printing of his plays. We now know that in some instances where a bad text was got hold of and printed, he did see to it that a proper, revised text was presented to the public. But the Company held the copyrights, the dominating considerations were the performing rights, which naturally they did not want to see spoiled by interloping printers. One such, Jaggard, did interlope to use Shakespeare's name and pirate some of his poems – and we learn that the author was much annoyed therewith.

Timon of Athens is full of the time, at home and abroad. Full use is made of the news of the gold-digging craze at Jamestown, where the first colonists were bent on searching for gold and neglected planting for food – and of course starved. 'Gold, precious gold! ... will make black white, foul fair, wrong right, base noble. This will place thieves, and give them title, knee and approbation, with senators on the bench.' True enough. The Jacobean peace saw the rise of new moneyed men to office and titles; the government even thought up a new order, the baronetage, to bring in revenue and appease the appetite for distinction. It was an age of vulgar ostentation – one sees it in the clothes, the absurd pompons on their shoes.

This is exposed in Timon's extravagance and inevitable bankruptcy, when he finds how false flattery and professions of friendship can be. 'Men shut their doors against a setting sun.' When Fortune changes and deserts her former favourite, his dependants who held on to him in his prosperity 'let him fall down, no one accompanying his declining foot.' Not one of his former friends will help, they all make humiliating excuses.

Among the flatterers appear a poet and a painter. Here is something new, for it reveals Shakespeare reflecting on the arts. The painter asks the poet, 'You are rapt, sir, in some work, some dedication to the great lord?' The poet replies, 'A thing slipped idly from me,' with the conventional deprecation one knows too well. 'What have you there?' 'A picture, sir.' He then enquires politely, 'When comes your book forth?' The poet replays polite interest: 'Let's see your piece.' He is ready with a compliment: 'This comes off well and excellent.' The painter: 'Indifferent', more self-deprecation. The poet enthuses: 'Admirable. What a mental power the eye shoots forth! How big imagination moves in this lip! The gesture one might interpret.' The painter, staking his claim: 'It is a pretty mocking of the life. Here is a touch: is it good?' The poet assures him:

> It tutors nature: artificial [artistic] strife
> Lives in these touches livelier than life.

Shakespeare would have heard such exchanges in the ante-rooms of the great, and perhaps among artists – though the only painter he mentions by name is Julio Romano, mentor of contemporary Mannerists. The interest for us is that it shows something of his own unprofessional idea of painting – that it should accord with, and be expressive of, nature. He concludes with a curious reflection: 'The painting is almost the natural man', and since man's nature is mixed, good and bad, 'these pencilled figures are even such as they give out.' As ever – no illusion.

Why did he not finish *Timon*? We do not know, but we have noticed that there was disarray in conditions at the time. The unfinished state of the play has a bonus for us: it reveals how in this instance, and probably others, he wrote up a scene as he saw it in the mind's eye, and jotted down the verses as they came – note the rhymed couplet that ends this scene. This was the regular conclusion to warn the audience in the absence of scenery changes. Other couplets appear haphazardly as they occurred to him. Some plays no doubt were written with a straightforward rush of inspiration, integral and homogeneous. *Romeo and Juliet* and *Othello* here come to mind.

The next play, *Pericles or the Prince of Tyre*, was also experimental and in the new direction, full of improbable adventures by sea and land. The motivation of the play was a story of incest, a theme which appealed to Jacobeans looking for something new to titillate audiences. The Master, however, played this down in favour of normal, natural bawdy, of which there is plenty.

What interests us is the part played by the poet Gower, Chaucer's contemporary, from whose chief book, the *Confessio Amantis*, Shakespeare took the form of the story. We know from the Sonnets that he had an eye for monuments – one of them refers to the big Southampton monument at Titchfield, which has the boy-Earl in armour upon it. In the big church, St Mary Overy in Southwark, the dominating monument was that of Gower, with his books piled up with him.

The observant eye of the Master missed nothing: he took up the suggestion to give Gower an important rôle as Chorus – much as he had done in *Henry V* to suggest off-stage action and to bridge time and space. He may also have given the writing up of this part in rhyme to a new recruit; or else the form in which it has reached us, from the quarto of 1609, was messed about in the disturbed printing-house conditions of that time. For the play proved popular, and may have been pirated.

Someone wrote that year of a crowd so long and loud 'that I truly thought all these came to see *Shore* or *Pericles*.' Ben Jonson commented grumpily that 'some mouldy tale like *Pericles* may keep up the Play-club.'

The last three acts, mainly in prose, are certainly Shakespeare's, the leading character here the chaste young Marina who, consigned to a brothel, resists all blandishments. We recall that on the South Bank close to the Globe were the 'Stews', a row of brothels conveniently near for popping into after the stimulant of a play. Marina, of course, was a precious tit-bit of a virgin – so, 'such a maidenhead were no cheap thing, if men were as they have been... There was a Spaniard's mouth so watered that he went to bed to her very description.' Marina holds out tantalisingly – for the audience too: 'Fie upon her! She's able to freeze the god Priapus... The pox upon her green-sickness for me! Faith, there's no way to be rid on't but the way to the pox.'

We may note how light-heartedly these writers took

129

the pox at the time. This was partly because the difference between gonorrhea and syphilis was unknown. They thought that they were two stages of the same disease – the first curable; or the second a 'bad', more severe case of the first, treated by hot baths, sweating, and the dangerous mercury treatment. Venereal disease was virtually a commonplace of the time, syphilis a world-wide epidemic, like Aids today.

This year 1609 saw at last the publication of the Sonnets, along with 'A Lover's Complaint', written so many years before. They were published not by Shakespeare but by Thomas Thorp, a rather highbrow publisher, who got the manuscript from Southampton's stepfather, Sir William Harvey Thorp, who wrote flowery dedications, called him the 'only begetter', not meaning inspirer, for that had been obviously the young patron. Unnecessary confusion has been caused by Thorp addressing him briefly and tactfully as 'Mr W.H.', for modern people who do not know that it was regular social usage to refer to a knight as Mr, i.e. Master. Actually in the Elizabethan House of Commons it was the regular rule.

The publication stung Emilia Lanier, and not unnaturally infuriated her, with its all too candid, indeed scandalous, depiction of her character. She at once announced the publication of the long poem she had in preparation, a notably religious work, biblical in inspiration, *Salve Deus Rex Judaeorum*. But for publication next year she inserted a leaf of prose answering the aspersions made upon her by men 'who – forgetting they were born of women, nourished of women and that, if it were not by the means of women they would be quite extinguished out of the world and a final end to them all – do deface the wombs wherein they were bred.' She called them 'vipers' – vehement and rhetorical as always.

Her book is very much in character, that of an educated woman, ambitious, proud, snobbish and tingling with resentment that she was not where she wanted to be. Her title page describes her as wife to Captain Alphonse Lanier, Servant to the King. When he had been on the Azores Voyage in 1597, with Southampton, she had gone to astrologer Forman to know whether she would be a lady of title, i.e. with Lanier knighted. He never was, and she went on to a series of quarrels and litigation with his family. (A brother became the ancestor of the American Laniers, while the Bassanos continued in England.)

Her book appeared with a galaxy of dedications to

the grandest of ladies, the Queen, Princess Elizabeth, Lady Arabella Stuart, and a number of Countesses most of whom she did not know. Susan, Countess of Kent, appears 'mistress of my youth'. At one time she had been befriended by the Countess of Cumberland, with whom and her daughter, she had spent a summer season at Cookham by the Thames. This formed the subject of an additional landscape poem. She was a fair poet, in addition to everything else.

What we should like to know about the Sonnets is why so remarkable a book was not republished for some years. Many editions of the poet's earlier poems of the same period, the early 1590s, had been called for. One can only suspect that someone stepped in to stay further publication until the poet and his former patron were safely dead. Neither of them could want the too revealing, often humiliating, story of their relations bandied about in public. The poet was now a famous man in his own right, the patron a prominent figure in government. Shakespeare was to die in 1616, Southampton in 1624.

Cymbeline was the play of this year, 1609. In its way it is also rather experimental, though the history-minded dramatist went back to the early story of

Britain and relations with Rome. Cymbeline recalled the British king Cunobelinus of Camulodunum, later Colchester. The play is oddly full of reminiscences of his early work – as if, in these years of suspension, plague etc., he had been re-reading some of it. Had the disturbing publication of the Sonnets reminded him?

We might interpose here to note that Plague – a regular returning feature of each decade – is regularly referred to in his work, Sonnets no less than Plays.

The motivation of the intrigue in this one is similar to that of *The Rape of Lucrece*: the wager here is laid by a husband that his wife would remain chaste in his absence. Tarquin is cited in a verse, the heroine Imogen is described in language that recalls *Venus and Adonis*. Also, 'she hath been reading late the tale of Tereus – where Philomel gave up.' This goes back to early *Titus Andronicus*, and she is also the 'rare Arabian bird' of 'The Phoenix and the Turtle'.

Various commentators have noticed a certain slackness in this overlong play, and some hesitations in the language. The admirable dramatic critic, Granville Barker, thought that *Cymbeline* showed signs of weariness, with sentiment rather than passion accounting for slack versifying. He thought that the country scenes were the best – might they have been written there?

133

Even the imperceptive Sir Edmund Chambers postu-
lated a possible breakdown of health. We are not at
liberty to make conjectures, but must stick to facts and
proper inferences from them.

The Master may well have had both the Globe and
Blackfriars in view, for the play does provide something
new – surprises, improbable turns, scenic spectacle and
an atmosphere of fantasy. In spite of the patriotic appeal of the British struggle against Rome, the patriotic
note is muted to 'our countrymen are men more or-
dered than when Julius Caesar' came. What a contrast
with the brags of Armada days! Observe the 'British'
ambience of the play – James I was keen to unify the
island as King of Great Britain.

And why, in the play, are the Romans made to land
at out-of-the-way Milford Haven, where they never did
historically? – Because this is where James I's great-
great-grandfather, Henry VII, had landed before his
victory against Richard III at Bosworth in 1485. So,
behind Cymbeline stands James I: he is the 'lofty cedar',
whose 'branches point thy two sons forth'. These are, of
course, Prince Henry and Prince Charles; the only
daughter stands for James's only daughter Elizabeth,
from whom our present royal family descends. The new
dynasty, 'jointed to the old stock', the Tudors, 'promises
Britain peace and plenty' – the best thing to be said for

James. No wonder he was as favourable to the drama-tist as Queen Elizabeth had been.

'A sad tale's best for winter,' he says. *A Winter's Tale*, of 1610-11, is not so much sad, as poignant, almost tragic, though all ends happily. It is in strong contrast to *Cymbeline*, for it makes a powerful integrated im-pact. It turns on the subject of Jealousy, with which Shakespeare was well acquainted: it formed the whole subject of *Othello*. 'Jealous souls are not ever jealous for the cause, but jealous for they're jealous – a monster born of itself.' In the new play Leontes fancied that he had a cause – his wife's evident friendship for his closest friend. In fact, pure obses-sion: his wife was chaste, but he drove her into exile and wrecked his family life.

Victorian critics thought the motivation unconvinc-ing. Shakespeare knew the dark recesses of man's mind better than they did. Today we recognise the dire consequences of obsession in schizophrenia, without the aid of Freud: Shakespeare knew it all already.

The charm of the play for us is in the scenes of country life – one would suppose it was written at home. We have a Cotswold shearing feast – half a dozen shepherds lived in Stratford. Here are the preparations.

'What am I to buy? Three pound of sugar, five pound of currants, saffron to colour the warden [pear] pies; nutmegs seven, a race or two of ginger; four pound of prunes, and as many of raisins.' Four-and-twenty nose-gays were made up, and three-mean songs laid on, but one Puritan among them and he sings psalms to horn-pipes.

There were to be country dances, and among them all comes in a thieving, engaging pedlar who sings his wares – people did in those days, as in the Cries of London.

> Will you buy any tape,
> Or laces for your cape,
> My dainty duck, my dear-a?
> Any toys for your head
> Of the new'st, fin'st, fin'st wear-a?

Remarkably we have an early recalling of himself among the home touches – why not? 'I thought I did recoil twenty-three years and saw myself unbreeched in my green velvet coat, my dagger muzzled.' *Coriolanus* had a touch of home in 'O let me clip [embrace] ye in arms as when our nuptial day was done and tapers burned to bedward.' Now we have a glimpse of a wife at home on a feast day, when she was 'pantler, butler, cook, both dame and servant, welcomed all, served all;

would sing her song and dance her turn…her face o'
fire with labour and the thing she took to quench it, to
each one sip.'

The age was one of music and song everywhere, in
town and country, palace, hall and cottage. This
playwright was the most musical of them all, and
wrote the loveliest songs for the stage. We should
note that music does not feature in the earliest plays
but increasingly from the time of his affair with
Emilia, of the professional Bassanos, Court musicians.

> How oft when thou, my music, music play'st
> Upon that blessèd wood whose motion sounds
> With thy sweet fingers…

Here she was at the virginals. No doubt her talent
was another weapon in her armoury of attractions –
not only for Shakespeare but for the elderly Lord
Chamberlain, who had a taste for music too, with
several compositions dedicated to him.

As for the Songs, they are perfectly placed in their
required settings and reflect the mood of the play. We
observe the development onwards, from the sprightli-
ness of *The Two Gentlemen of Verona*:

> Who is Silvia? What is she
>> That all our swains commend her?

and the gaiety of *As You Like It*:

> Under the greenwood tree
> Who loves to lie with me,
> And turn his merry note
> Unto the sweet bird's throat?

On to the melancholy note of *Twelfth Night*:

> What is love? 'Tis not hereafter…

along with the drunken catches of Sir Toby Belch, the play ending with folksong. We move to the moodiness of *Measure for Measure*:

> Take, O take those lips away
>> That so sweetly were forsworn.

Ophelia's broken heart and Desdemona's desolation are expressed in their songs. Ariel's songs are perfect in character for a sprite:

> Where the bee sucks, there suck I,
> In a cowslip's bell I lie.

V. Blackfriars Again

Most haunting of them all:

> Fear no more the heat o' the sun
>> Nor the furious winter's rages,
> Thou thy worldly task hast done
>> Home art gone, and ta'en thy wages.

Surprisingly, in next to the last of his plays, a phrase of Marlowe's surfaced – after all those years – welling up in that incomparable memory, an actor's memory:

> Come unto these yellow sands,
>> And then take hands,
> Curtsied when you have and kissed –
>> *The wild waves whist…*

That last line is Marlowe's.

Many remarks in the plays testify to what he thought about music: for him, in the first place, invariably associated with love. 'If music be the food of love, play on – give me excess of it.' Or, 'Give me some music – music, moody food of us that trade in love.' The man that has no music in his soul is fit for anything questionable, and not to be trusted. Again, 'how sour sweet music is when time is broke and no proportion kept!' Perhaps most revealing personally is this reflection on its varying powers on us: 'Music oft hath such a charm to make bad good, and good provoke to harm.' This sounds a note of personal experience, reminiscent of what we may guess.

In May 1612 Shakespeare made an appearance in the Court of Requests at Westminster to give evidence in a suit concerning the Mountjoys of Silver Street, where he had lodged about 1602 – or before. Here he is: 'William Shakespeare of Stratford-upon-Avon, *gentleman*, of the age of forty-eight years or thereabouts.' All correct. The Mountjoys' son-in-law, one Bellot, another Huguenot, formerly an apprentice, had married their daughter and was suing them for dowry, promised but not delivered. Their former lodger, with his usual good will, gave the apprentices good characters. What is interesting to us is that he was on terms of confidence with Madame Montjoie, for, on her behalf, he had betrothed the young couple with a ring. He could not remember further details about the amount of the dowry, etc. The authorities of the Huguenot church did not give the menfolk of the house a good character: '*tous deux débauchés*'.

The Court hoped for more evidence from the former lodger, but at a further session he was not forthcoming, away in the country.

V. Blackfriars Again

From these last plays it would seem that he was more at Stratford, for they are full of country life and lore and nostalgic country scenes. With this year's play, *The Tempest*, he was responding yet again to a topical event, and in a complete way for the whole play was moulded on it. His imagination was touched by those most notable events, the Atlantic voyages, the settlements in the New World, for he read up the leading authorities, Sir Walter Ralegh, Richard Hakluyt, Richard Eden.

In 1609 the colonising voyage, headed by the new Governor, met with a hurricane, in which the flagship foundered on the coast of Bermuda. The ship broke up, but not a soul was lost. Crew and colonists saved the timbers to build a pinnace to finish their journey in the spring. They landed provisions, the island provided plenty of fish, fowl and wild hogs. They must have had an interesting time of it.

An account of it all came back to Blackfriars from William Strachey, who was secretary of Virginia, which Shakespeare read and used for details – notably details of the hurricane, 'St Elmo's fire' running down the rigging etc. Contemporaries thought that the island was haunted, 'full of noises' and sprites. All this and more spoke to the imagination and resulted in one of the most beautiful of all plays. We have the engaging sprite, Ariel, and the disagreeable monster, Caliban, a new creation playing on the word 'cannibal'. He represents Shakespeare's reaction to the (later) cult of the 'innocent savage', the sympathy with primitive society initiated by Montaigne. Caliban is far from an innocent child of nature, he is mischievous, cunning and resentful, plots against the order established by the exiled Duke and to ravish his virginal daughter. For all his soaring imagination Shakespeare was down-to-earth, knew too much about human nature to entertain illusions.

He read Montaigne's optimistic, doctrinaire views of society in the recent translation by John Florio, his old acquaintance in Southampton's household. And indited a punishing caricature of such a 'commonwealth', in which everything was to be done by 'contraries', contrary to common sense, we perceive. 'No kind of traffic, no name of magistrate – Letters should not be known.' We remember his early caricature of Jack Cade rebelling against lawyers and learning, schools and writing. The commonwealth is to be paradisally communist – 'riches, poverty, service none; contract, succession, bound of land, tilth, vineyard, none. No use of metal, corn or wine, or oil. No occupation: all men idle – and women too, but innocent and pure. No sovereignty. All things in common nature should produce without sweat or endeavour.' In this blissful state there would be no treason (or treason trials? no

purges?). 'Sword, pike, knife, gun, or need of any en-
gine' – all unnecessary. Nature would bring forth
plentiful harvests and abundance 'to feed my innocent
people'. (See Communist Russia!)

An innocent enquires, No marrying among them?
To which the answer is given: 'None, man: all idle,
whores and knaves.'

We see that no amount of imagination could seduce
him from common sense. His own uphill struggle
against circumstances and misfortunes had taught him:
'they well deserve to have who know the surest way to
get.'

Why was his last completed play, *Henry VIII*, so different from what had gone before? In one sense it
was a reversion to his earlier plays dealing with English history. But this was a more recent, tetchy
subject, a hot potato to handle. For Henry VIII was
a controversial character. Nothing could be said
about him in the reign of his daughter Elizabeth,
whose innocent mother, Anne Boleyn, he had executed (in reality because she could not provide a male
heir to the throne any more than Catherine of
Aragon did).

For the grand espousals of James I's daughter Elizabeth to Frederick, the Elector Palatine on the Rhine, in 1613 many plays were produced, about half of them Shakespeare's, among them the new play. King James hoped to balance this Protestant marriage by marrying his son and heir to a Catholic Spanish Infanta. Henry VIII's Spanish marriage was relevant, but offered a thorny problem – its end in divorce. How to deal with that, and retain good will with Spain? Once more we see how necessary it is to know the historical, topical circumstances to which the most successful dramatist, favourite of the Court, geared his plays.

He could always be trusted to be tactful, and to handle such problems with ease. Here it is done by putting the blame for the divorce on Cardinal Wolsey, and making the loyal and patient Catherine the heroine of the play. The warm-hearted Dr Johnson (finest of Shakespeare critics) thought her character the most beautiful of all feminine parts in the Plays. Henry and Anne are reduced to lay figures. Cardinal Wolsey has the most memorable male part: he is depicted with touching sympathy, after all, in his fall from power. He had enjoyed 'the world, the power and the glory', and his part has appealed to leading actors ever since.

The event of the baptism of Henry and Anne's daughter, by Archbishop Cranmer, gave Shakespeare the opportunity to pay a noble tribute to the great woman who was to give her name to the Age, of which he has handed down to us the fullest mirror. 'She shall be a pattern to all princes living with her.' This was no more than the truth, admitted as much by Pope Sixtus V as by the Protestant Henri IV. The poet balanced the courage with which she had fought foes abroad with the internal peace and safety her rule had maintained – 'in her days every man shall eat in safety under his own vine what he plants.'

Her successor is likewise praised – as he deserved for his peace-keeping; with the addition that he shall 'make new nations' – here Jamestown and Virginia are fore-shadowed. 'He shall like a mountain cedar, reach his branches to all the plains about him.' Here is again the 'cedar' of *Cymbeline*, which the attentive reader had noticed in Ralegh and Hakluyt's accounts of Virginia. We may remark that Shakespeare was quite as much the favourite dramatist of those monarchs as Racine and Molière were of Louis XIV.

From his buying the Blackfriars property in 1613, half the gatehouse into the upper-class precinct, he clearly was not retiring from his theatrical interests. He had provided for the succession there with the recruitment of Beaumont and Fletcher, and also

Massinger, to write for it. What is remarkable is how much their work owed to the Master: several of their plays are inspired by reversing the story or the intrigue of one of his plays. Such was the 'miraculous fecundity' – as someone has put it today – of his mind: imagination, invention, reflection. All these were stimulated by the challenge, the conflicts of character, the contrarieties of events, on stage. No less was the inspiration – as to any writer – of both personal experience, and that of others, and of that soaring age.

Again it does not seem that he was giving up from Stratford evidences. He paid a business visit to London in the company of his son-in-law, Dr John Hall. When he made his will in March 1616 he was 'in perfect health and memory'. It looks as if he was carried off in April by a sudden illness, perhaps an epidemic, leaving certain loose threads – most important the publication of his plays.

In undertaking this posthumous task his colleagues, Heming and Cundall, did an exceptional, indeed a magisterial job. It was a tremendous project, reproducing thirty-seven or so plays, some half of them from manuscript. It involved several publishers, took seven years, and did not appear until 1623, the year of his widow Ann's death. She desired ardently to be buried in the same grave with him. His Fellows of the Company testified that 'what he thought he uttered with that easiness that we have scarce received from him a blot in his papers.' We might have guessed the speed at which he wrote. By contrast Ben Jonson was a slow, constipated worker: even his songs he wrote in prose first, than translated them into verse. His was a ratiocinative, critical intellect, rather than inspirational.

Shakespeare's will gives a clear picture of his circumstances at the time. He died, as he had lived, a conforming member of the Church, with the Protestant formula of hoping for salvation through the merits of Jesus Christ, not the Catholic formula through intercession by the Virgin Mary and the Saints. He left money for rings to remember him by to Heming, Cundall and Richard Burbage. All the rest of the will is family and Stratford, and is very neighbourly: there are a dozen or more neighbours remembered by Stratford's chief townsman, the gentleman of New Place. His ultimate heir was his granddaughter Elizabeth. Note that this was not a Shakespeare or Arden family name – another tribute to the sovereign who meant so much to him? This last sprig eventually became a titled lady, Lady Barnard of Ablington in Northamptonshire. In his day those things mattered.

More important for our purpose is what Ben Jonson thought, who knew him so well. Though a critical spirit and apt to be grumpy, Ben was capable of affection and critical generousness. He evidently found William a loveable man. We should observe closely what he has to tell us in his tribute prefaced to the big First Folio when at length it appeared: 'To the Memory of my Beloved, the Author, Mr [i.e. Master] William Shakespeare, and What he hath Left us' – that is, both to the man and his work. He begins by hailing him as 'The Soul of the Age! – the applause, delight, the wonder of our stage! Thou art alive still while thy Book doth live.'

He then compares his achievement with his predecessors: 'how far thou didst our Lyly outshine, or sporting Kyd, or Marlowe's mighty line.' This offers a precise critical summary in brief space. He had surpassed the early sparkling Court comedies of Lyly, and the impact of Kyd in tragedy exemplified by his famous *Spanish Tragedy*, which long held the stage (and probably an early version of the Hamlet story, transcended by – in my view – the greatest play in the world's dramaturgy). He then went on to challenge 'Marlowe's mighty line'. This is exact criticism again, for Marlowe's achievement had been to marry the finest poetry to the drama. His rival went even further here too – and people have been slow to recognise the soaring literary ambition that led him on. It seems clear that Greene had an early inkling of it.

Ben Jonson's bias was in favour of the classics. It is therefore all the more remarkable that he rated Shakespeare along with the grandest spirits of ancient Greece and Rome. He called forth 'thundering Aeschylus, Euripides and Sophocles, for the comparison of all that insolent Greece or haughty Rome sent forth.' He then expresses patriotic pride for Britain, not only for England (for Ben was of Scottish descent):

> Triumph, my Britain, thou hast one to show
> To whom all scenes of Europe homage owe -
> He was not of an age but for all time!

This proved singularly prophetic – astonishing, coming as early as it did in yet only 1623.

Ben went on from the achievement in tragedy to that in comedy, comparing him with 'the merry Greek, tart Aristophanes, neat Terence, witty Plautus' – Shakespeare's starting point in this field. Ben does not single out the large corpus of plays inspired by history – English, Scottish, Roman and otherwise – though nearly half the plays were historical in inspiration, for in those days they were not regarded as a separate

genre. Today an eminent medievalist has called Shakespeare, surprisingly, greatest of historians, and the great
Duke of Marlborough confessed that all the history he
knew came from Shakespeare.

Ben Jonson continued with a salutary emphasis on
the aesthetic side, for Shakespeare has often been ab-
surdly regarded as an untutored child of nature. 'Yet
must I not give Nature all: thy Art must enjoy a part –
for though the poet's matter Nature be, his art doth give
the fashion', i.e. the form -

> For a good poet's made as well as born.

This simple principle is overlooked in the torrential
character of this poet's inspiration. Though his bent
was not classical like Ben's, he could provide his own
versions of a classic kind in *Julius Caesar* and *Coriolanus*, for his genius was universal. Here the
philosopher Santayana reinforces Jonson: 'Nature is
the moving ground of experience, and experience a
play of moral counterpoint or conscious crosslights
upon the surface of nature.'

The philosopher continues with an observation
which we may apply to the man William Shakespeare:
'A life should be harmonious with itself, in a distinct
form in which all the parts are included without being

distorted.' Ben concludes with the man in his profession:

> Sweet swan of Avon, what a sight it were
> To see thee in our waters yet appear
> And make those flights upon the banks of Thames
> That did so take Eliza and our James!
> Shine forth, thou Star of Poets!...
> ... I see thee in the Hemisphere
> And made a Constellation there!